Key Knowledge for Success

Words of Wisdom

Barbara D. Culp

Glean knowledge and wisdom from the experiences of someone who has successfully traversed the roads of education. Written for educators and learners in all walks of the educational journey, Words of Wisdom provides a collection of guiding principles, practical advice, and encouraging words for both beginners and veterans in the world of education.

Other Titles in This Series

Vintage Knowledge for Principals: Keys to Enrich, Encourage, and Empower School Leaders and Empowering Today's Principals
Essential Knowledge for Teachers: Truths to Energize, Excite and Engage Today's Teachers
Trusted Knowledge for Parents: Tips to Prepare, Position and Empower Today's Parents
Choice Knowledge for Students: Words to Empower, Enliven and Enrich Your Life

Key Knowledge for Success

Solutions to Augment, Fortify, and Support Today's Superintendents

Barbara D. Culp

ROWMAN & LITTLEFIELD
Lanham • Boulder • New York • London

Published by Rowman & Littlefield
A wholly owned subsidiary of The Rowman & Littlefield Publishing Group, Inc.
4501 Forbes Boulevard, Suite 200, Lanham, Maryland 20706
www.rowman.com

Unit A, Whitacre Mews, 26-34 Stannary Street, London SE11 4AB

British Library Cataloguing in Publication Information Available

Library of Congress Cataloging-in-Publication Data

Names: Culp, Barbara D., 1947- author.
Title: Key knowledge for success : solutions to augment, fortify, and support today's superintendents / Barbara D. Culp.
Description: Lanham, Maryland : Rowman & Littlefield, 2017. | Series: Words of wisdom | Includes bibliographical references and index.
Identifiers: LCCN 2017000183 (print) | LCCN 2017015238 (ebook) | ISBN 9781475835861 (electronic) | ISBN 9781475835854 (pbk. : alk. paper)
Subjects: LCSH: School superintendents—United States. | School management and organization—United States. | Educational leadership—United States.
Classification: LCC LB2831.72 (ebook) | LCC LB2831.72 .C85 2017 (print) | DDC 371.2/011—dc23 LC record available at https://lccn.loc.gov/2017000183

∞ ™ The paper used in this publication meets the minimum requirements of American National Standard for Information Sciences Permanence of Paper for Printed Library Materials, ANSI/NISO Z39.48-1992.

Printed in the United States of America

School superintendents occupy a special place in every community because of their selfless drive to provide the best education possible for their district's children.

This book is dedicated to the thousands of school superintendents across the globe who lead with integrity, guide with commitment, and serve with the best interest of all children at the top of their agendas.

"Character cannot be developed in ease and quiet. Only through experience of trial and suffering can the soul be strengthened, ambition inspired, and success achieved."—Hellen Keller

"He who cannot be a good follower cannot be a good leader."
—Aristotle

Contents

Foreword

> We can, whenever and wherever we choose, successfully teach all children whose schooling is of interest to us. . . . There has never been a time in the life of the American public school when we have not known all we needed in order to teach all those whom we chose to teach.—Ron Edmonds

Every hopeful superintendent candidate undergoes a daunting selection process. Whether the candidate is a newcomer to the career or an experienced professional, meeting the challenge marks a milestone in a superintendent's professional life.

During the preparation process, the prospective candidate clears hurdles and presents the best he or she has to offer. Still, nothing prepares you for the moment the contract is signed. With the stroke of a pen, the full responsibility for a school district falls on a single pair of shoulders: your own.

To fulfill the demands of this position, you must become a culture changer. Every company and group has its own culture, a collective way of approaching the lives and activities of each individual within that group. Your district also has a culture, one that is made up of the values and beliefs of every student, teacher, and citizen in the district.

This culture determines the behavior of staff, students, administrators, and parents. When the existing culture produces excellence and supports the academic needs of the schools, your job is to maintain and enrich that culture. In cases where the culture doesn't support academic excellence or, at times, when divisiveness threatens the district's stability, the superintendent must meet challenges head-on.

It all starts with a vision. You, as the leader, must create a vision for the district that leads everyone toward the goals. Then you must transmit that vision to all the different groups involved with the district. Once everyone comes on board, the students and the community benefit.

Key Knowledge for Superintendents is a rich toolbox filled with everything you'll need for the path ahead. Dr. Culp's broad background and respected experience will show you how to set goals, reach milestones, and celebrate the accomplishments of your district. It will prevent small bumps from becoming overwhelming obstacles. Best of all, it will show you how to take any district into the realm of excellence.

Read this now. Whether you're just starting out or have a wealth of experience, add this book to your professional library. Place it on the corner of your desk where you can read through it again and again. Dr. Culp's warm and enlightening wisdom will help you every step of the way.

Dr. J. Jerome Harris
Former School Superintendent
Atlanta Public Schools

Preface

I'm going to be blunt here. During my decades in education, first as a teacher and as a principal for one of the largest elementary schools in my district and later as a superintendent in training, I never once saw a superintendent who did everything right.

Now, before you start thinking that my assessment is brutal, consider that superintendents are human beings. No one is going to do everything right all the time. And in a job that requires 24/7 access, constant juggling of resources, ever-shrinking budgets, and the creeping threat of political or public blowback, the ways to make a misstep are far too numerous to count. No human being can undertake that kind of career and expect to be perfect!

So, before we even begin, allow me to offer you one very important piece of advice: be kind. Be kind to others who have no idea what it takes to do your job every day. Be kind to peers and administrators who are suffering under similar workloads. Be kind to community members who can't scrape together the resources to offer the support your schools really need.

Most of all, be kind to yourself! Take the time you need to refresh and recharge. Have a strong network of friends you can turn to in those moments when you need to talk. Spend a lot of time with your family so that your soul is fed by the same benefits that trickle down through your schools to other families.

And for heaven's sake, give yourself a break when it turns out that you can't do everything right! Mistakes happen. Most, you'll find, can be alleviated or corrected. Always remember that the media or public criticism can blow tiny missteps way out of proportion, so it's important for you to maintain a balanced view. And consider the source. If individuals or groups who don't understand how your district operates come after you or one of your staff, stand firm. Be proud of who you are and the services you provide to your district.

Stay focused on the good: the good your efforts are doing for the schools, the great education being provided to students, and the superior professionals who are teaching in the classrooms and managing the campuses. Welcome every opportunity to achieve something more. And celebrate! Every rise in test scores and every dollar saved is another point in your district's favor.

There will be many missteps, that is true. There will also be milestones of triumph. You will have weeks, even months, when operations are running as smoothly as a ship on glassy seas. No matter what happens during the school year, the parade of graduates across the stage at year's end walk on the foundation of your successes. Every smile on a parent's face, every job worked by a graduate, and every volunteer effort that helps your community and your schools is another brilliant gem to store up in your heart.

The job of school superintendent will challenge you at every level of your being. It requires that you call on a lifetime of experiences inside and outside of education. It asks that you become the very best that you can be in order for the schools to grow. It demands that you hold firm to the values and vision you have for the district even when those values and that vision are challenged.

You will be called on to innovate and inspire. You will need to pull together factions that hope never to speak to one another. When you step up to the challenge of being a school superintendent, you must harness your faith, your focus, your intuition, and your intellect for the singular goal of academic achievement. When you do succeed—and you will succeed—you will create a bright and prosperous today for the schools and a shimmering future full of opportunity for your students.

Thomas Edison said, "Nearly every man who develops an idea works at it up to the point where it looks impossible and then gets discouraged. That's not the place to become discouraged."

When you sign on as a school superintendent, you already know what lies ahead of you. To others, the task looks impossible. But to a trained professional with the heart and courage and compassion to do what is best for a district, nothing is impossible!

So grasp that wheel with all the confidence the board has shown in placing you in such a powerful position. Assess the waters using the skills and training that have proven you worthy. Steer through the shoals with the steady strength of wisdom. Power your district through the waves with the stability of your knowledge.

When you arrive at the port of each goal, you'll deliver a cargo of academic treasures to the community of staff, parents, students, and teachers. And then, using this book as your map, you'll sail out again!

Acknowledgments

As an educator with decades of experience, I would like to acknowledge all the individuals—teachers, parents, administrators, staff, and school communities—who work together to build districts that are truly great.

Among these individuals, each of whom is important in his or her own right, the district superintendent stands alone. Every moment of every day, superintendents reach out to their communities to nurture relationships with—and between—other individuals and groups. Every action they take helps a parent, a student, a teacher, or a citizen support the community and the schools embedded in that community.

The job of a superintendent isn't easy. It demands that every skill be utilized to its fullest degree. When superintendents rise to the call, the legacy they create lasts for lifetimes.

Introduction

As the leader of your school district, you are responsible for a host of activities. On any given day, you might hire a principal, approve an educational program, adjust the budget, delegate tasks, meet with the board, chat with parents, and reach out to the larger community. In fact, you can count on doing a little bit in each of those areas every day!

The whole time you're juggling these various activities, you must engage the influencers who impact district operations, keep the board informed, align activities with goals, and ensure that the vision for the district remains clearly visible to everyone involved. Every bit of your effort must move the schools closer to the goal of academic excellence.

Yours is a complex role with a complex history. When public education first came into being, the lead teachers were in charge of their own schools. These principals were governed by a group known as the select committee. Eventually, the states began to provide funding for public education, and the responsibilities expanded to encompass the county level.

The first state superintendent of education position was officially created in 1802 in New York. Over the next sixty-five years, a few dozen cities set up their own superintendents. Not until after the Civil War did population growth spur the hiring of superintendents by school boards across the country.

During the beginning of the twentieth century, superintendents had exceptional control of their districts. Most school boards handed them the reins and allowed them to manage as they saw fit. Then, in 1965, the Elementary and Secondary Education Act indicated the federal government's interest in exerting more control.

The authority that had once been held by a single individual was dispersed among a number of groups and individuals. That same situation holds true today, especially in the area of public scrutiny. Yet the superintendent is still the chief executive officer who is expected to be a superior instructional leader, an educational visionary, an efficient communicator, and an effective manager.

To meet these expectations, you must display compassion, wisdom, forethought, and ability in equal measures. This book, which is packed with advice based on real-world experiences, is a must-read for those who aspire to or currently serve as a district superintendent. Your role is pivotal to every school's effort to aim higher and reach farther in mastering the art of teaching and learning.

Key Knowledge for Success is here to help! In this book, we'll look at your role as a superintendent and the leadership you can provide to students, parents, peers, administrators, and the community. Techniques that have proven effective will be discussed. Best of all, you'll be supported in all the areas you handle every day of the year.

Key Knowledge for Success provides relevant and necessary information in three separate categories: "Superintendents in the District," "Superintendents as Professionals," and "Superintendents as Leaders."

In the first section, entries like "Leap across the Gap" and "Equality Equals Excellence" will provide guidance on real changes that can close the education gap. "Tech Talk" and "Building a Blog" will expand your digital capacities, while "Call on the Children" and "The Wheel of We" ensures that everyone in the district is able to pitch in.

The second section focuses on your leadership with entries like "Powerfully Wield Power" and "Manage Mandates." Advice that can help you reach higher in your career is covered in discussions like "Ask an Attorney" and "Interrogate the Interview." Managerial and operational elements are discussed in entries like "Early Wins" and "Strategic Direction."

The final section focuses on the ever-important political and diplomatic aspects of your duties. "The Door Is Now Open" encourages feedback while protecting your valuable time. "Ace Accountability" and "Continuity Counts" will help you pilot your way through daily activities, while items like "The Ethical Shepherd" spread your influence in positive and proactive ways.

Because each entry is concise, this book can be read straight through or in sections. Fast, effective implementation tips steer you toward a district in which student achievement is in step with district goals, parents are supportive and satisfied, and the community is eager to applaud the district's performance.

Everything in this book is intended to make your job easier and support your district's core responsibility. Every tip is based on my fifteen years of experience as a teacher and an educational leader. When I think about the awesome responsibilities that come with the position of school superintendent, I must commend the courage, fortitude, and confidence of those who take on the challenges that face today's educational leaders.

Remember that you occupy a special place in every community. Your selfless drive to provide the best education possible for your district's children serves our nation and our world. It's an awe-inspiring responsibility. With *Key Knowledge for Success* in hand, you'll live up to that responsibility efficiently, effectively, and with true confidence and power!

"Historical Development of the Public School Superintendent." ELearnPortal.com. Retrieved from http://www.elearnportal.com/courses/education/school-system-administration/school-system-administration-school-committees.

"Superintendent of Schools—History, Importance in Education, New Expectations, an Evolving Role." *Education Encyclopedia.* StateUniversity.com. Retrieved from http://education.stateuniversity.com/pages/2471/Superintendent-Schools.html.

Part I

Superintendents in the District

VENTURE OUT

Venture out into the district to ensure that you (and your position) are visible!

Venturing out ensures that everyone involved with the schools knows who you are and what you do. You serve teachers, students, parents, and the community at large, all while interacting with the board. When people recognize you and understand your role, the channels of communication stay wide open. And since that is always a two-way street, you will be able to capture support for your initiatives!

Superintendents who venture out comfort the district in important ways. At every level, people recognize that their superintendent cares enough to visit their PTA meetings and stop in at individual schools—even when things are going well! You present yourself as a leader who is open, flexible, and ready to help. The personal touch is a powerful touch!

Venture out a few times a month at a minimum. Your normal duties will take you out of your office to meetings with different groups. Add your own handful of special stops whenever you can. Pop by events to cover a lot of bases at once. A few minutes spent watching a football game from the sidelines will allow you to chat with a few parents, a couple of students, the coach, teachers, and possibly even that school's principal. Plus, you'll enjoy watching the teams play!

CONNECT WITH THE COMMUNITY

Connect with the community to encourage engagement and community partnerships.

Connect with the community to discover the values held in your district. Build trust by building an open and direct line to the people who are impacted by every decision you make. Then, when the time comes for you to call on their support, you'll be able to reach out directly and strategically to the individuals and groups who can offer you the strongest support.

Connecting with the community is vital for a superintendent's success. Doug Bassett, who served as superintendent of a medium-sized suburban district in the Midwest, noted that the position is often recruited from outside the community. That can lead the community to viewing the superintendent as a "tourist" or an outsider. With those types of dynamics built into the position, it's especially important for you to connect with your community multiple times and build real, lasting connections.

Connect with the community on social media. It's surprising how few districts do this because those that do reap enormous benefits. Use social media to tell stories gathered from around the district. Rather than posting only when there's a triumph, follow each story from its inception all the way to the end. You can even use social media to replicate a more personal form of interaction by posting pictures of you and your staff. Write personal notes about your day's progress and allow your staff to do the same. You'll find that it's nearly as powerful as shaking hands and chatting in person!

Dymond, Judith A. "Strategic Community Engagement as Perceived by Five Superintendents." National-Louis University. 2014. Retrieved from http://digitalcommons.nl.edu/cgi/viewcontent.cgi?article=1086&context=diss.

MAKE THE MOVE

Make the move to your district's county so that you are integrated from day one!

Make the move to your district's county to place yourself in the heart of your new community. When you live with the people who are affected by your job, you learn about the daily issues that everyone from the students up to the administrators face. You'll benefit from meeting the people who are involved in the schools on a friendly basis. And you'll create a network you can call on whenever you need assistance!

Although *making the move* means leaving behind colleagues and associates in one place, it opens up new opportunities. One of them is the type of benefits you might receive, like the transfer of or a cash payment for unused sick days. Your kids might benefit because they end up in a superior school! Best of all, though, the associates you leave behind will still be available for certain types of assistance. Overall, your network grows!

Make the move as seamless a transition as possible. Try to get into your new home before the school year starts so that you can learn a little about the local lifestyle. While packing, make sure to keep the things you'll need right away separated so that they can be accessed immediately. Plan for plenty of outings for you and your family so that everyone feels comfortable in their new environment. And if your kids are really young, tap the local PTA for the names of reliable babysitters. You'll be glad to have someone handle the kids while you unpack or just take a break with your spouse!

CALL OUT THE CURRICULUM

Call out the curriculum to develop a rigorous and comprehensive approach.

Calling out the curriculum ensures that all aspects of education are regularly assessed and enhanced. This ensures that you are meeting learning standards and objectives and that the district's focus supports those elements. From individual courses to entire programs, calling out the curriculum allows you to plot a path to success!

Call out the curriculum to ensure that every teacher is heading in the right direction. Frequently, individual teachers develop their own curriculum that is refined each year. They use packages provided by companies, items garnered from peers, and their own judgment. Superintendents can guide the teachers by sending out a list of objectives for each subject along with a list of resources.

Call out the curriculum on a regular basis. Make the beginning and end of each school year a time when teachers and administrators assess their curricula. Once these assessments are finished, ask each school to provide your office with the results, including specific comments. Then share that wisdom between schools by compiling everything into a single document that is delivered to every teacher and administrator. By pooling these assessments, you'll generate ever more powerful results!

PROMOTE PROGRESS

Promote progress to create continuous and sustainable improvement.

Promoting progress gives every individual in the district a way to get involved. It rewards star performers by calling them out as examples that can be imitated, and it encourages low performers by showing them that everyone can make progress. When the results are shared with the community, parents and students discover valuable information that is usually kept behind the scenes. They feel included in every element of the district's operations.

Promote progress to become a true leader. Superintendents who ask for and share this type of information prove that they are capable, practical, and professional. The community recognizes that the persons at the top hold themselves ultimately responsible for everything that happens, which inspires trust.

Promote progress by using the tools already at your disposal. Ensure that the assessment and accountability procedures generate accurate and fair feedback. Integrate the necessary tools to collect data, analyze the information, and draw conclusions about the district's next step. Look always toward how things can be improved, even with programs that seem to be running well. Promote progress to promote your entire district!

TECH TALK

Tech talk uses technology to support teaching and learning.

Tech talk explores and promotes the most effective and appropriate technologies for education. Using the devices that best fit your district's needs will transform students, teachers, administrators—and even yourself! You'll create lifelong learners and enable teachers to become lifelong educators.

Superintendents who engage in *tech talk* send a clear signal: they are leaders in innovation. The best technology leaders are curious, observant, and flexible, all of which reflect the core components of a superior academic approach. And since social media make up such a wide-ranging element of technology today, supervisors who talk tech model their own recommendations! Nothing garners more confidence in others than a superintendent who takes his or her own advice.

Tech talk might involve a lot of different types of devices and programs, but the core vision is always clear: a singular focus on enhancing academic achievement. Digital literacy tools can help English as a Second Language (ESL) students close the language gap more quickly. Kids with socioemotional challenges have a digital path to learning that bypasses the stress of interacting with adults or peers. Best of all, technology provides a number of ways to track, measure, and assess progress!

LEAP ACROSS THE GAP

Leap across the gap in achievement by challenging your staff!

Leaping across the gap ensures that every student receives a solid education no matter their background, race, ethnicity, socioeconomic status, or gender. Grade-point averages rise, standardized testing becomes inspirational, dropout rates plummet, and college enrollment increases. The pride that parents and administrators have in your schools shoots through the roof! Everyone wins—most of all, the young minds in your care.

Superintendent Tony Evers in Wisconsin aims to *leap across the gap* with a step considered controversial in the predominantly white state: talking about how race impacts a student's grades. He notes that African American and Hispanic students from wealthier families, despite the socioeconomic advantage, still often achieve at lower levels than underprivileged white children. In addition to the emphasis on earlier and better education in math and literary subjects, Evers recognizes that the most successful method is to build relationships between students and educators, between peers, and between staff and parents.

Leap across the gap by focusing on equity. Strong relationships between teachers and students enable kids to feel comfortable asking for help—and make it easier for students to accept help when teachers broach the subject. When students know that their teachers and the rest of the staff care, they know that they are valued for who they are and the abilities they already possess. That spurs an even greater passion to learn! That passion resonates with parents, who will want to become more involved, and with the community, which will benefit from students who are prepared to become productive citizens.

CHART THE CHARTERS

Chart the charters to keep all the schools in your district on track!

Charting the charters will track the very real impact that charter schools can have on traditional schools within a single district. Since the impact blends positive and negative effects, you'll be able to minimize the negative elements and enhance the positive ones. A proactive approach also encourages the two types of schools to work together more often for the benefit of all!

Charting the charters keeps you in touch with opportunities that might not be available without the presence of charter schools. In Atlanta, for example, Superintendent Meria Carstarphen proposed to close some schools and turn others over to charter groups as a way to address the city's worst schools. She felt that her sweeping and sudden changes would be the best way to help the students rather than allowing them to be managed by the state. Since the move will potentially increase funding in coming years, it's a unique response to a situation that otherwise would have had no happy ending.

Chart the charters by networking with the administrators and the unofficial leaders of charter schools in your district. Study their curriculum offerings each year to see if traditional schools shouldn't add programming or change existing offerings. Consider whether their teaching methods might work well for specific subsets of public school students or even the entire population. Encourage schools to mirror what works for the charters as well as to learn from their mistakes.

SYNC THE SCHEDULE

Sync the schedule of your district to that of surrounding districts to garner a trove of benefits!

Syncing the schedule of your district to surrounding districts helps the community stay in sync with your schools. Volunteer efforts are going to be much more successful if parents and local businesses are asked for help during the time when they're accustomed to volunteering. Students appreciate breaks that come when their friends have breaks, and teachers appreciate being able to vacation with neighbors and nearby relatives.

Sync the schedule to ensure that enrollment numbers stay at the level you want. If your schools are too far out of sync with neighboring districts, parents who want to enroll their kids in your district are going to have a much tougher time making that transition work. Your schools might end up with fewer students or become overburdened with students who can't get into other institutions. Keeping a balance in the number and types of students enrolled keeps the budget balanced!

Take the opportunity to *sync the schedule* when the state reorganizes the districts. Consider the times when breaks are offered, the length of breaks, and the times when the school day starts and ends. Your district doesn't have to match others exactly, but the schedule should make sense compared to others. Also consider whether to shift the schedule for special programs, like pre- and postholiday events, parent meetings, and even presentations by after-school groups. Try not to plan events on days when other districts tend to offer their own, and you'll end up with more support from vendors, community groups, and families who have children enrolled in different districts.

ALTERNATIVES BEFORE SUSPENSION

Superintendents who develop *alternatives before suspension* make their schools more effective.

Alternatives before suspension eliminate policies that tend to unfairly penalize students with socioemotional challenges as well as those from minority ethnic groups. They also address the failure of suspension to address inappropriate behaviors or to prevent them. Finally, alternatives ensure that the students who need the most help aren't left behind by absences.

Alternatives before suspension will make your schools better! Districts that develop alternative responses create a more caring and compassionate climate inside the school and in the community. The relationships between students and teachers and between teachers and parents become much less contentious. Parental involvement increases, issues are handled before they spin out of control, and students feel that the system is fairer.

Develop *alternatives before suspension* by pulling together the resources your schools already have. Encourage teachers to use the time between classes to hang out in the hallway so they can be available for students. Utilize the counselors as much as possible by telling students they can visit even if their problems don't seem all that important. Consider implementing a program that catches students being good and offer rewards, like pencils with the school's logo or recognition in the community bulletin. Every one of these alternatives makes your district an emotionally—and academically—safe harbor!

EXPAND CULTURAL CAPACITY

Expand cultural capacity to ensure that all students can grow!

Expanding cultural capacity ensures that minority and underprivileged students as well as those with disabilities and ESL learners achieve academically. When awareness and inclusion initiatives take center stage, the entire community will pitch in! Teaching strategies that are culturally responsive develop leaders and good citizens who will build a better future.

Superintendents who *expand cultural capacity* improve their districts and the wider world. Cultural capacity initiates lower dropout rates, increases on-time graduation, and guides more students into college. When students who have been given these benefits graduate, they take a huge step forward because they are better prepared for adulthood.

Expand cultural capacity by training every teacher in your district on culturally responsible strategies. Ensure that the books in the school libraries and classrooms represent a true variety of nations and lifestyles. Team up with local colleges and universities to create conferences that offer fun, informative programs geared toward higher education. Invite business leaders and parents to speak during a lyceum for a unique career day program that presents students with familiar faces.

PUBLIC RELATIONS ARE POWERFUL RELATIONS

Public relations are powerful relations because they keep the community informed and inspired!

Public relations are powerful relations, especially in today's world. A community that is informed about the protocols and operations of the district will trust in the ability of the schools to provide a sound education and a safe environment. Teachers and other staff will feel validated and valued, and the top performers from other areas will be drawn to your district. The public image you build over time will support your schools when things get tough.

Superintendents who make *public relations into powerful relations* win in the communication game! The media are powerful influencers of public opinion. The district's public image is key to ensuring that tax dollars flow your way, that volunteers step up when needed, and that issues are handled calmly. The most important benefit might be that you will be viewed as the leader you were hired to be!

A handful of simple steps can make *public relations powerful relations*. Consider hiring a media or communications expert at least part-time to manage the district's communication needs. Be proactive about getting information out to the community before they hear about it from a different—and potentially corrupted—source. As with financial investments, the more you put into public relations, the greater your returns! Keep the focus on communication, information, education, and achievements. Stay positive, stay transparent, and you'll engage in a powerful way!

KNOW BEFORE YOU GO

Know before you go prepares you for those occasions when your feedback will be solicited—even when you're not on the docket!

Know before you go so that you stay comfortable and confident in any situation. Your presence at conferences, meetings, and group discussions stands out—and so will your words. When you prepare a short statement for every situation, you present yourself and your district as capable and informed.

Apart from the times superintendents officially have to *know before they go*, they will frequently be called on at informal gatherings. Parents, the community, and school officials are so accustomed to hearing from superintendents that it's natural to call on them in the moment. Being asked to comment off the cuff is also a sign of respect for your position and the value you provide in your role. Recognize this and know what will be best for the district before you step into those situations!

Know before you go doesn't entail preparing a scripted speech. Instead, think through how you might address the issue if you were called on officially. Select the most important point and talk about only that. In a few brief sentences, you will have contributed an important voice to the conversation. And since you prepared, you'll appear confident in your own words and inspire confidence in others.

DELVE INTO DETAILS

Delve into details to ensure that you know exactly what should be happening in each department.

Delving into details will save time in the long run. When you first step into your role, review the tasks assigned to each department. Over time, you can measure their actual performance against those mandates and make adjustments before things go too far off course. And when requests for additional resources come in, you'll know whether the requests are appropriate as well as whether they're actually required.

Delve into details with the learning materials used by your districts. This will give you insight into the various departments responsible for instructional standards, learning assessments, programming requests, and student achievements. These details will also guide your consideration of workshops and other opportunities that teachers and school administrators might want to attend. A baseline understanding of different elements of the schools will resonate with a number of your tasks!

Delve into details by occasionally reviewing operating procedures. This allows you to make adjustments to tasks as varied as scheduling, maintenance, and daily operations. It isn't necessary to memorize a ton of details or even to read entire manuals. A working knowledge of the overriding principals and goals of each department will be enough to supercharge your district's performance by making your every decision hit the target!

INNOVATE TO INSPIRE

Innovate to inspire the district's staff and to support your goals.

Innovate to inspire staff through different activities and events, and you'll pull everyone together to work toward the district's goals. During these events, you'll build teamwork, engage the faculty, inspire new ideas, and create a deeper sense of community. Because these elements are so critical to meeting goals, you'll fire the passion of every individual!

Superintendents who *innovate to inspire* get the best from their district. A simple example is to change staff meetings so that they address only those elements that have a meaningful impact on students. Everything else—all the minutiae of different activities, all the administrative tasks—can be handled through social media or other communication channels.

Innovate to inspire at every level inside your district. Encourage the use of live streaming tools to better engage staff during meetings. Put teachers together in a room and have them act out the funniest encounter between themselves and a student and then end with the lesson they learned as a teacher. Invite parents to attend a mixer with their kids where everyone wears a costume of the person they most admire. Once people let their creativity loose, you'll spark a revolution that results in connections, passion, and a lot of fun!

SHARE THE WEALTH

Share the wealth by publicly recognizing specific schools and individuals.

Share the wealth to validate the efforts and accomplishments of the organizations and people in your district. Being appreciated is valued by everyone and results in satisfaction and increased productivity. The motivation to continue doing good work or to excel beyond even those levels increases. The district is caught in an upward spiral!

State superintendent Tom Torlakson *shared the wealth* when he stopped by a Redwood City elementary school he thought could be a model for other schools in California. Roosevelt Elementary had won an academic excellence award for its efforts to lift the performance of students from disadvantaged communities. Principal Patricia Girardi was so touched that she was moved to tears!

Share the wealth by touring classrooms that are challenged by the neighborhoods in which students live. Offer the students a few words about your own struggles to inspire them to reach high! Send thank-you notes to the parents of top performers and students who are making significant progress. Offer teachers who stand out a gift card for their local café. And always remember to thank the personnel you work with every day. A little recognition goes a long way!

Walsh, Austin. "Top State Educator Recognizes Local School." *The Daily Journal.* September 13, 2016. Retrieved from http://www.smdailyjournal.com/articles/lnews/2016-09-13/top-state-educator-recognizes-local-school-state-superintendent-touts-roosevelt-elementary-as-model-for-excellence/1776425168199.html.

HUSH

Hush, and you'll listen in a way that returns big rewards.

When you *hush*, you open the way for others to communicate exactly what's on their minds. You'll learn more about the topic as well as the person—their opinion, their reasoning, and possibly even their motivation for bringing up the topic. Plus, you'll convey respect for that person and everything he or she stands for. Nothing helps you more than being a great listener!

Hush is so important to Los Angeles Unified Superintendent Michelle King that she went on a "listen and learn" tour to help her put together a plan for the district. "It's about all of us," she said. "It's going to be done from the ground up." And the only way to know what the parents and students on the ground needed was to hush and listen.

There are times to talk and times to *hush*. Finding that balance can depend on the type of situation you're in. When you're attending a meeting but aren't slated to speak, use the time to ask a lot of questions. For those times when you are slated to speak, leave time afterward to create informal connections with attendees. Let people know ahead of time that you'll stick around afterward so they can plan. These little steps can make a big difference in how your district views your office as well as your performance as its chief executive.

Kohli, Sonali. "Superintendent's 'Listen and Learn' Tour Leaves LAUSD Parents with Questions Unanswered." *Los Angeles Times.* May 26, 2016.

CHARISMA CAN MOVE MOUNTAINS

Charisma can move mountains because it relies on effective communication and emotional trust.

Charisma can move mountains because individuals are truly inspired by a charismatic leader. Superintendents who communicate well and prove themselves trustworthy garner the loyalty and passion that makes the impossible possible. Education clearly needs that type of power!

Charisma can move mountains for superintendents. Great leaders are effective because charisma is a positive characteristic. Leaders who can connect directly with individuals power them toward the district's goals. The individuals become motivated to band together and bring the common vision to life. Nothing is more powerful!

Charisma can move mountains, but how can superintendents become more charismatic? Recognize that ego-driven traits are not the same thing. Strike the negative elements, like boastful pride, and share credit for the efforts others have made. Project confidence even—and especially—when the chips are down. Remain steadfast while pursuing the goals for your district, and you'll rarely fail to woo others with your charisma!

GET THE GRANT

Get the grant to invest more funding in your district and your schools.

Getting the grant can shore up budget shortfalls that come when cutbacks hit areas your district needs for peak performance. Grants that offer multiyear funding can ease the worries that might result from one-time grants or budgets that are constantly under political fire. Finally, grants give you the freedom to innovate in ways that can have long-ranging impacts!

When superintendents from three different areas in Virginia *got the grant* that provided $3.5 million for STEM (science, technology, engineering, and mathematics) courses, their middle school students were the big winners! Using the grant, existing engineering classes were funded at larger levels. Since these are the types of initiatives that catch the eyes of universities and colleges, the districts set their students on a bigger, brighter path to success.

Get the grant for everything from new textbooks to tablets and security equipment. Look into grants according to whether your school is urban, suburban, or rural. Use your student and community demographics to locate private companies that fund educational initiatives based on their mission statements. Finally, be sure that the principals and teachers in your district are allowed to apply for small grants. The extra money can fuel a real renaissance at the grassroots level and trickle back up to your office!

Thomas, Loren. "Superintendents Announce $3.5M Grant for Innovation in Schools." CBS 19. January 30, 2015. Retrieved from http://www.newsplex.com/home/headlines/Superintendents-Announce-35M-Grant-for-Innovation-in-Schools-290361371.html.

DITCH THE PAST

Ditch the past because the way you did things at your previous district might not fit your new district!

Ditch the past to stay focused on the future. Releasing prior attitudes, ideas, and preferences clears the deck for innovation and growth. Best of all, resources that would normally be consumed in maintaining the status quo become available. By jumping the historical track, you leap into a bold new frontier!

Ditching the past has worked very well for Washington High School in Canton, Ohio. The school's district decided to get rid of old ways by changing the library into a media center. Outdated reference materials and underused books were donated to a public library. Meanwhile, the old library now offers Chromebooks on which students can work, a thirty-two-foot projection screen, and Wi-Fi. No one has complained, but everyone has gained!

Ditch the past by throwing out anything that harms the students and the schools: overly aggressive suspension policies, year-end finals that consume too much effort compared to the benefits, and even letter grading can be eliminated in favor of more effective and efficient methods. No matter how many new things you welcome, be sure to resurrect old methods when appropriate. Try using paper testing instead of the state's digital forms to reduce the number of glitches that penalize students!

Knapp, Amy L. "Washington High School Library Ditches Traditional Use for Media Center." Canton Rep. January 28, 2016. Retrieved from http://www.cantonrep.com/

news/20160127/washington-high-school-library-ditches-traditional-use-for-media-center.

THE WHEEL OF WE

The wheel of we pulls together everyone in the district so that effort equals effect!

The wheel of we builds a circle of active influencers by placing every individual in the district on the wheel of doing. Whenever you speak about the efforts and programs being undertaken by your office, emphasize the teamwork created by the shape of a wheel! Every individual will work harder to reach the goals because the wheel is always rolling forward.

Superintendents who focus on *the wheel of we* build an environment where the group—the schools in the district, the parents and students, and the teachers and administrators—are encouraged to put in their best efforts. Districts that place everyone in the same boat nurture the diversity and fairness that allow the district to reach its goals!

The wheel of we shifts the dynamic from one in which power accrues only to the superintendent to one in which power is distributed more evenly. When individuals are empowered to become their best, they take up the torch that sets academic achievement ablaze! Encourage collaborations between parents and teachers. Pull together groups (and individuals) who tend to have contentious interactions for a common cause. Spread the credit wherever and whenever it's due and assign individual mission statements to specific groups to enhance buy-in. Whenever that wheel turns, the power of we carries all the students forward!

THE HOME-TEAM ADVANTAGE

The home-team advantage utilizes a team of advisors cultivated from among your contacts.

The home-team advantage is key for effective leaders. When you cultivate a team of advisors, you have a built-in accountability mechanism against which to check actions you're considering. The team will also be among the first to listen to new ideas, so they can bring up problems you might not foresee. Best of all, they can keep you motivated because they will fully support the best ideas and opportunities for your district.

Having *the home-team advantage* is like having your own coach—or coaches! Just as athletes rely on coaches to guide them to peak performance, your team will ensure that your performance is always running at maximum capacity. They will help you with the behind-the-scenes work that can't be shared with anyone else. And they will broaden your perspective by giving you their take on any issue or program being considered.

Cultivate *the home-team advantage* by selectively building a team of advisors starting with your immediate contacts. Having individuals close at hand gives you the added benefit of an extra set of eyes watching how things spool out day by day. Be sure to include individuals who are not in your district. Sometimes a perspective that stands at a distance is the one that shows you the best path! With a capable team of advisors available, you'll be more confident making decisions about issues that have to be settled right away. You'll be much less likely to take a wrong step when you combine your expertise with that of others.

SET AN ACADEMIC TONE

Set an academic tone throughout your district so that everything is done with the students in mind.

Setting an academic tone keeps the focus on your number one priority, which is the students. Improvement and achievement become a natural by-product in districts that maintain an attitude that emphasizes academics. Best of all, students educated in a truly academic environment become lifelong learners who aspire to college!

Once an *academic tone is set*, ripples spread throughout your district. Every teacher is held to high standards alongside their students. Parents recognize that their participation is not optional! People buy into data-gathering initiatives because having a yardstick that measures improvement is clearly important. The atmosphere in every classroom becomes one of professional scholars who develop a love of learning and who become capable, impassioned citizens.

Set an academic tone by aligning the curricula with the assessment process. Ensure that teachers see how student improvement and performance affect their reviews. Coordinate professional development opportunities at every level and embed opportunities for parental involvement in every school's operations. Track every student demographic to ensure that they are growing in a dynamic way. Engage every person at every level, and the academic tone will chime with your district's success.

ACHIEVEMENT IS NONNEGOTIABLE

Achievement—among students, teachers, and administrators—*is nonnegotiable.*

When *achievement is nonnegotiable*, your district is spurred to become the absolute best. Academic achievement and continuous improvement is expected from every student no matter where they start out. Teachers must achieve by guiding their students, principals must achieve by leading the teachers, and your own leadership achievements crown them all! Even parents must achieve by supporting their children's academic efforts.

Achievement is nonnegotiable even in districts plagued with violence. A study performed for the National Institutes of Health in 2013 found that while violence negatively impacts test scores, it doesn't negatively impact grades. Since the effect was linked to cognitive stress and classroom disruptions, the study found that teachers are able to counter these effects. Superintendents who provide teachers with the resources to form warm, supportive relationships with their students truly support academic achievement.

Prove to your district that *achievement is nonnegotiable* by being its best champion! Fight against every dollar politicians want to cut from the budget and be proactive in recruiting donations from businesses. When teachers ask for new instructional methods, listen to their logic! Give each principal the authority to operate in ways that best fit their student population. And call on parents to help with homework, monitor their child's attendance record, and expand their learning opportunities at home. When achievement is nonnegotiable, you lift up your entire district!

McGill, Tia M., Self-Brown, Shannon, Lai, Betty, Cowart-Osborne, Melissa, Tiwari, Ashwini, LeBlanc, Monique, and Kelley, Mary Lou. "Effects of Exposure to Community Violence and Family Violence on School Functioning Problems among Urban Youth: The Potential Mediating Role of Posttraumatic Stress Symptoms." U.S. National Library of Medicine National Institutes of Health. February 7, 2014. Retrieved from https://www.ncbi.nlm.nih.gov/pmc/articles/PMC3916821.

BANK POLITICAL CAPITAL

Bank political capital so that when you need to cash in, you have a large amount in savings!

When superintendents *bank political capital*, they shore up their district by piling up human resources. City councils and other minor political groups can help navigate issues originating in state and federal governments. Business owners and managers can provide financial and material resources for different projects. Social workers and health care providers can be a great resource to address student needs.

Superintendents who *bank political capital* make deposits in the "favor bank." By doing favors for key influencers inside your district, you set up a savings account your educators and leaders can withdraw from when the time comes! Businesses need future employees, and the community relies on the graduates who emerge from your schools in many ways. Every time you bank political capital by reaching out and helping those groups, you remind them of the debt they owe the district for its ongoing efforts.

Bank political capital from day one. The moment you arrive in your new district, join the local chamber of commerce. Locate parent-focused groups and attend their meetings at least once a quarter. Set up intern programs that provide university credits to reach current professors and future professionals! Keep the media informed of all the great things your teachers and students are doing so that they can fulfill their mission to inform the community. Every minute you drop into the bank of political capital will pay rich dividends!

SYMBOLS TO RALLY AROUND

In any district, *symbols to rally around* supercharge academic achievement!

Symbols to rally around are those actions you take that speak volumes. Every classroom visit tells students and teachers that you care about what happens in their world. When you participate in a principal's performance evaluation, you signal the value you place on their position and their role. Dropping in on a PTA meeting clearly conveys your desire to connect with parents. With each act, you become the ultimate symbol around which the district will rally!

When symbols are tied to specific activities, they become *symbols to rally around.* Consider how the presence of the American flag works in classrooms across the nation. It is a reminder that the United States is hoping for the best for every student and teacher; it also reminds students of their obligation to achieve their best! How powerful it would be if every school in your district created its own flag around which to rally!

A superintendent's behavior and attitude are the primary avenues to building *symbols to rally around.* Although you're in charge, encourage your personnel to become self-actualizing by talking about any issues that prevented you from achieving your best. Connect each of your schools with a school in a different state and one in a different country so that your students take pride in the school they represent. Create ceremonies that celebrate the educational values held by the district's teachers and administrators. Focus on the meaning of these actions, and your district will have an anchor of hope!

THE COMMUNITY IS IN CHARGE

The community is in charge of everything from meeting district goals to academic achievement.

When superintendents allow their district's *community to be in charge*, they leverage the 75 to 80 percent of citizens who might not have school-aged children. Because the entire community has a stake in education, this voting bloc can have a profound impact on the amount of resources that become available to your schools.

When *communities take charge* of their district, both the schools and the students reap the benefits. A study by Steven Constantino measured data for four years at a high-achieving school. During the study, communication with parents became a primary focus. As a result, parents became more involved. The average SAT score shot up sixty-one points, and the education gap dropped by 18 percent! The dropout rate also fell from 11 to 3 percent.

Encourage your *community to be in charge* by reaching out to everyone—not just parents. Every resident of your district is a stakeholder interested in building a brighter future, so make sure they have the information they need to cast the votes that support education. Task your communications officers with creating a plan that spans the entire year. Aim for quarterly updates at a minimum. As your outreach builds over time, you can consider whether monthly updates might be beneficial. An informed community is your best ally!

National School Public Relations Association. "Eleven Tips for Savvy Superintendents." February 2008. Retrieved from https://www.nspra.org/files/docs/SavvySuperintendents.pdf.

KNOW WHO YOU'RE TALKING TO

Know who you're talking to in order to have the greatest impact in your district.

Knowing who you're talking to allows you to adapt your communications to fit the target. Parents might want to hear very different things about your schools than business owners, so tailoring the message avoids confusion. A targeted message also prevents recipients from feeling burned out by education updates that don't apply to them. When you know who you're talking to, you'll be able to keep their attention on the issues that need their support!

Knowing who you're talking to can have an impact on funding. The National School Public Relations Association (NSPRA) reports that the most consistent voters who cast their ballots for school finance issues are over forty-five years old. The NSPRA also reports that, most of the time, over 50 percent of the people who vote in a school election are over the age of sixty. Your district can't afford for you to overlook those voting blocs!

Know who you're talking to by looking into the demographics for your district. Determine the economic profiles, poverty estimates, geographic data, and other demographics using the U.S. Census Bureau's data on school districts. State governments and governors' offices usually keep similar statistics, and the state's information can be more up to date than that of the Census Bureau. Websites, like Movoto, and real estate companies are also useful because they often utilize maps and other graphics. Once you know who's living in your district, you'll know exactly who you're talking to!

National School Public Relations Association. "Eleven Tips for Savvy Superintendents." February 2008. Retrieved from https://www.nspra.org/files/docs/SavvySuperintendents.pdf.

BREAKING NEWS

Have a system that provides *breaking news* to parents and key influencers.

Breaking news to the community and key influencers goes a long way toward avoiding misunderstandings. In crisis situations, the community will recognize that the situation is already being taken in hand when they hear it from the superintendent's office first. By ensuring that the breaking news system is accessible to principals and the board, you make communication more effective and efficient.

Breaking news must be given to the community by the superintendent's office or a similar high-level administrator. When parents hear something disturbing from the press, they wonder why the district hasn't already informed them—which leads to suspicion and doubt. Employees at all levels also need information delivered within the same quick time frame so that they can handle issues before they get out of hand.

To effectively *break the news*, set up a data bank of templates. Include messages that address sudden or extreme crises, letters intended for parents, letters intended for the entire community, and so on. Provide a list of addresses for each important group: parents, teachers, administrators, community influencers, and the board. These templates allow your "first responders" to quickly inform the appropriate groups with messages that have already been vetted and approved. Your office won't be stalled by efforts to communicate at a time when it really needs to focus on managing the problem.

BUILD A BLOG

Build a blog to engage the entire district in a direct and friendly way.

Building a blog can provide you with a megaphone that reaches into every household in your district. Blogs are a great tool for superintendents because they provide a format that can be used for short messages or longer posts. You'll increase transparency, connect more directly with people you might never meet in person, and create a more human portrait of the person at the top!

Many public relations specialists encourage superintendents to *build a blog*. Campus Suite, a company of education website specialists, notes that superintendents are sometimes hesitant to begin one. They fear that they will say the wrong thing or wonder what they might blog about. With a focus on school triumphs and student accomplishments, any superintendent can post knowing that his or her blog will be uplifting!

Build a blog by deciding how you want to focus your posts. Your blog can be a mix of things that vary according to the calendar and school or student progress. You might also decide to have a blog that posts only once a week or every two weeks, which is usually a better fit for a narrow focus. Invite teachers and students to submit photos from their special events or things they do every day. Adding a picture can really enhance the impact of the blog. Since pictures also increase the number of times a blog post is shared, they can help you gain traction!

Brant, Kathy. "5 Steps to Launching a Superintendent's Blog for Your School District." CampusSuite.com. December 11, 2014. Retrieved from https://www.campussuite.com/5-steps-launching-superintendents-blog.

HELP THE HOMELESS

Help the homeless students in your district provide a safety net for their education.

Helping the homeless ensures that all the district's students will thrive. Because the stresses involved with being homeless can result in behavioral issues, helping these students will ensure that classrooms retain an atmosphere in which all the children can learn. Additionally, superintendents will ensure that their schools adhere to any legislation set down by local authorities around education for homeless students.

Helping the homeless is more important today than ever. The National Center on Family Homelessness reports that homeless students are four times more likely to have delayed development. They struggle with learning disabilities at twice the average rate and are twice as likely to repeat a grade. Absences and school changes are a key part of the reasons why they need to repeat a grade.

Help the homeless in your district by providing for needs that revolve around their education. Ensure that every school has a place where homeless students can store their books and personal belongings. Reach out to the community for ride-sharing programs that allow students to travel from shelters or other areas that aren't on the bus line. Allow them to use the showers in the gym and set up an annual drive to collect personal care items, like deodorant and toothbrushes, for homeless students and their families. With these simple steps, you'll provide support that means the world to a homeless child!

Bassuk, Ellen. "Ending Child Homelessness in America." *American Journal of Orthopsychiatry* 80, no. 4 (2010): 496–504.

SMART ECOSYSTEMS

Smart ecosystems create an environment in your district that focuses on education.

Smart ecosystems pull together all the resources and individuals in your district for the singular goal of education. When parents, business owners, and higher education institutes are treated as real partners, students swim through an educational ecosystem even when they're not in school!

A *smart ecosystem* has helped Promesa Boyle Heights create a connected system that links educators, students, and various community groups. The Alliance for a Better Community helps serve the Latino community. Centro de Ayuda provides services that build social, emotional, and economic self-sufficiency. And City Year develops young leaders and promotes good citizenship. Together, these partners are transforming the Boyle Heights district!

Build a *smart ecosystem* by seeking out nonprofit groups that serve individual demographics inside your schools. Recognize that organizations that serve adults can support the parents in your district, so be sure to tap those groups as well. Build summer programs that bridge the break and implement projects that help grade-schoolers transition to high school before their first day in the upper levels. A smart ecosystem is a smart choice!

Promesa Boyle Heights. "Our Partners." Retrieved from http://promesaboyleheights.org/our-partners.

EQUITY EQUALS EXCELLENCE

Equity equals excellence because all students receive the same opportunities.

Equity equals excellence without arbitrarily raising standards. True excellence supports the academic achievement of all students regardless of race or socioeconomic conditions. Providing equity also fosters an environment in which every person is offered the respect they deserve. Nothing is more important to the student than knowing that he or she is valued!

In Nashville, Tennessee, *equity equals excellence*. PASSAGE, the Positive and Safe Schools Advancing Greater Equity initiative originating at Brown University, is building a coalition among the district's stakeholders. These include principals, parents, counselors, teachers, law enforcement, clergy, community leaders, researchers, juvenile judges, and government officials. By bringing everyone together in a steering committee, they aim to create a more positive school environment.

Implement the attitude that *equality equals excellence* by providing ways for different stakeholders to work together. Bring them the issues at hand and ask for their cooperation. Have one or two baseline program ideas in mind so that they have a starting point on which to build. Socioemotional learning, positive interventions, and after-school support can go a long way toward spreading the equality within your schools to every neighborhood!

Annenberg Institute. "School Discipline Equity: PASSAGE (Positive and Safe Schools Advancing Greater Equity)." Retrieved from http://annenberginstitute.org/what-we-do/projects/school-discipline-equity-positive-and-safe-schools-advancing-greater-equity-pass.

CALL ON THE CHILDREN

Call on the children to get their perspective on how initiatives impact the classroom experience.

Calling on the children is the ultimate in customer service! When the district asks the primary users—students—about their experiences in the classroom, the answers are going to be honest and straightforward. Even when very young children can't express themselves well, they can indicate their level of engagement by saying what they like and dislike. You might be surprised what this feedback tells you!

State Superintendent Richard Woods of Georgia *called on the children* to set up a student advisory council. Using the community newsletter, he asked for middle and high school students to serve on the council. During the year, they met directly with the superintendent to discuss how state policies impacted their classrooms. They were also free to bring up other issues. They served as ambassadors in their different schools and connected Woods directly to the classroom!

Call on the children by setting up an advisory council in each school. For grade levels that might be too immature to handle an official group, utilize less formal methods, like having teachers poll their students with a single question every month. Allow every student to provide feedback through their school's advisory committee. The district can also hold votes that allow students to cast ballots for or against certain programs or ideas. When you open up the floor to the people your district serves, you'll engage students on an entirely different level!

Georgia Department of Education. "State School Superintendent Richard Woods Seeks Student Advisory Council." August 1, 2016. Retrieved from http://www.gadoe.org/External-Affairs-and-Policy/communications/Pages/PressReleaseDetails.aspx?PressView=default&pid=456.

CONTEXTUAL DEVELOPMENT

Contextual development offers professional development opportunities related to the district's context.

Contextual development provides a positive experience for educators and administrators. The needs of staff in rural, urban, and suburban districts are going to change according to student and community demographics. When professional development opportunities are tailored to match the context in which the staff work, the district achieves excellence on its own terms!

Contextual development is all about the circumstances inside your district—and only your district. The emotional and psychological counseling needs of a district that has suffered from an extremely violent event is going to be very different from a district that has never once been touched by such an intense crisis. Considering the context of the past and the present will guide your district into its best future!

Ensure that *contextual development* opportunities reach your staff by understanding the circumstances under which they operate. In addition to the budgetary constraints and community demographics, consider events that have impacted the school and the surrounding neighborhoods. Negative events can be alleviated by allocating new resources or forming community partnerships to deal with the effects. Positive events can be strengthened by ensuring that the steps taken to create that event are repeated. When professional development opportunities that fit the context are offered, staff are better able to deal with daily realities.

Part II

Superintendents as Professionals

POWERFULLY WIELD POWER

Powerfully wield power by being thoughtful about your every edict.

When you *powerfully wield power* with forethought and compassion, the people you need on your side respond with loyalty. Because your team knows that you won't abuse your position, they trust that even the most difficult challenges you place before them are for the district's good. Everyone from parents to principals will do what it takes to reach your targeted goals!

The best superintendents *powerfully wield power* and achieve the most. Superintendents who set easy goals or take the path of least resistance might have lackluster results. Ones who are bold, however, set the bar higher. Achieving those challenges happens much faster—and with far less pushback—when you have established a track record of thoughtfully using your position to achieve specific targets that benefit the entire district.

Power can be wielded powerfully through your attitude and your approach. Return the trust that individuals have placed in you by allowing your people to do their jobs. And when someone isn't working up to snuff, address the issue directly and with compassion. Find the best route forward for every challenge, even when the obstacles seem insurmountable. You'll inspire everyone to go beyond because you hold the power and you use that power responsibly.

HOPE AND PLAN

Hope and plan to cover a wide range of outcomes so that you will always be prepared.

Hope and plan means that you hope for the best outcome while planning for less optimal (and even the worst) outcomes. The hope keeps you and your entire district moving forward and focused on the future. Planning for suboptimal outcomes ensures that no matter what, you will always have a way to keep things rolling. When you hope and plan, students receive everything they deserve!

Superintendents who *hope and plan* recognize the realities inherent in their jobs. Education has always been challenging; in today's changing environment, it has become ever more so. Superintendent Cindy Elsberry of Horry County Schools in South Carolina hoped for the best when she turned her attention to selecting the types of devices students should use. The sheer number of choices was overwhelming. When she stepped back to consider how best to plan for the choice, she recognized that personalized learning was more important than the type of device. She was then able to make the best decision for her district by planning her decision and hoping for the best outcome!

Hope and plan in equal measures. Place your best efforts into creating an optimal outcome. Then consider the types of obstacles that might arise. Plan for funding shortfalls by having unique options for fund-raising in your back pocket. Head off technology issues by offering training to all educators in the devices. Recognize that undiscovered learning needs will crop up in student populations every year and have a list of resources on hand. Hope for the best and plan for workarounds to keep your district operating smoothly no matter what!

Roscorla, Tanya. "5 Education Problems That Superintendents Face." *Converge.* Center for Digital Education. April 2, 2014. Retrieved from http://www.centerdigitaled.com/news/5-Education-Problems-that-Superintendents-Face.html.

PICK YOUR PLACE

Pick your place in a rural, suburban, or urban district to create the best match.

Superintendents should *pick their place* to ensure that the district they end up managing is one where they can succeed. The differences between running each type of district can be huge, so understanding how they are different is important. A well-informed choice will ensure that your career and your district thrive!

When superintendents *pick their place*, often they turn away from rural districts. The challenges facing these schools can be significant: isolation, limited resources, and community resistance to change are some of the top problems. But rural doesn't always equal small. A larger rural district might allow you to take action more easily than in a small urban or suburban district. And because a rural superintendent is often the sole person in charge, the rewards could be greater than at a district where you have to bend to the dictates of others!

Pick your place by researching the differences between rural, urban, and suburban schools before you start to apply. Rural communities can offer less of a private life, which could be perfect for a highly social superintendent. Suburban districts can offer larger talent pools for educator positions, but they might also result in higher turnover rates as individuals seek out better opportunities. Urban schools, which are known for having a host of difficulties, could be the exact challenge you need to inspire your best performance! Know before you look, and you'll parse each opportunity according to your own abilities and needs.

SELF-EVALUATE

Self-evaluate to ensure that you are fulfilling your role to the best of your ability.

Self-evaluation is invaluable for superintendents. No one knows what you do better than you, and that means that no one can evaluate your performance as well as you can! Self-evaluation gives you the opportunity to catch small issues before they become big problems. It can also provide you with an overview of your accomplishments—and that will spur you to even greater heights!

When superintendents *self-evaluate*, they go deeper than the board's evaluation ever could. Rather than looking only at the legal requirements that the board has to follow, self-evaluation can go deep into motivation, intent, and approach. While reaching performance goals is important, when you self-evaluate, you can consider the intangible areas that impact your performance. Examine all the subtle elements, and you will surely shine!

Self-evaluate by setting up a regular time for this process every month. Start by pulling up the weekly to-do lists for that period. Scan individual items to see how many were finished. For each week, write down a sentence about what could have gone better and how you could have accomplished greater results. Also write down one sentence that lays out why tasks that showed sterling results were so successful. Over time, you'll discover patterns that point to your strengths and areas where you need to pay a bit more attention. As little as an hour at the end of the month can reap a lot of rewards!

INTERROGATE THE INTERVIEW

Interrogate the interview that you will complete in front of the board.

Interrogate the interview to leave the board with a lasting impression of your professionalism and your dedication. Utilizing effective interview techniques ensures that your abilities and your ideas come across clearly. When you communicate well in this situation, you create trust in the one group that has the greatest impact on all your efforts for your district.

It's especially important that superintendents *interrogate the interview* because each board will modify or change the questions it asks according to the issues faced by its district. So, while you can be sure that your discussion of problems and solutions will be assessed, you also want the board to assess your professionalism. When you utilize good interview techniques, you avoid the pitfalls that can make even sterling superintendents appear less than capable.

Interrogate the interview by considering the questions that most boards will ask. Questions about a candidate's prior job, motivation, and role in the community are favorites. Boards also frequently ask about the standards the supervisor will use to judge the effectiveness of everything from the board of education to policies and parental complaints. Most boards delve into your style of management as well as your views on curriculum. Be prepared by thinking through brief, informative responses, and you'll sail past the other candidates!

LIBERAL OR CONSERVATIVE

Superintendents who know whether they are *liberal or conservative* stay ahead of the game.

Superintendents can be *liberal or conservative*. Knowing which one you are will help you find the right groups and individuals to support your efforts. And when it comes time to working with other educators, understanding how you and the other person might differ can help you move forward no matter how far apart you stand.

When politics in a county shift from *liberal to conservative* or vice versa, superintendents can get caught in the crossfire. Boards that turn out to be a superintendent's polar opposite can snarl the implementation of new procedures. They can even slow the progress of activities that are already in place, and they certainly might turn the community against their district's chief officer. Recognizing who you are and where your board and district stand can help you circumvent this type of trouble!

Ensure that *liberal or conservative* issues don't overwhelm the benefits provided to students by focusing always on the schools. Keep your comments low key. You might hold personal beliefs that tend toward certain directions, and that's everyone's right. As long as the school, the students, the parents, and the community will benefit, that's the most important element! Keep your attention there to encourage others to keep their attention there—no matter whether they are liberal or conservative!

MANAGE MANDATES

Manage mandates to ensure that your district meets or exceeds state requirements.

Managing mandates provides your district with the benefits that the state hopes will come from its requirements. Because many parents are aware of state mandates, meeting or even exceeding them will enhance their trust in you and your abilities. When the going gets tough, teachers and administrators will rally behind you because you have delivered consistently.

Supervisors are required to meet mandates, but *managing mandates* is a much better approach. When you meet them, you're just doing your job. When you manage them, you involve the board, the parents, key staff, and influential people or groups to help you meet them. Managing mandates allows your schools to come in under budget, meet goals earlier, and lift their students and the community to higher levels.

Manage mandates by looking at the impact each mandate will have on your schools. For example, state testing requirements will impact every student, so be sure that at-risk students have the resources they need to make the grade. If one school is consistently spending "too much" per student because their population has greater needs, garner support for that population through the community. And whenever a mandate is exceeded, be sure the entire district knows about that triumph! Success breeds success—and pride!

MEASURE STRESS

Measure stress to prevent burnout and to keep your enthusiasm alive!

Measure stress throughout the year. When you hit a particularly rough patch, you can look back and compare your current stress level to the typical day—and perhaps discover that things aren't so bad! By constantly tracking stress levels, you'll be able to foresee difficult periods and pull in additional support beforehand. You'll also become aware of times when you really need a break.

Measuring stress is key for career longevity. Ongoing high levels of stress will make you feel embattled, underappreciated, and overworked even when the individual issues aren't actually all that terrible. Keeping tabs on your stress level allows you to step away for a few minutes or a few days to recharge. By measuring and managing stress, you'll be much better equipped to manage your district!

Measure stress with your day calendar. At the end of each day, pop an emoticon onto the calendar or draw a quick doodle. Use a thumbs-up for a great day, a neutral face for an okay day, and a pig for days that just didn't go well. The act of adding a cartoon figure to your calendar will also help you develop a lighter perspective! When you get too many pigs in a row, you know it's time for a change. Either get some help or plan a short break. A long lunch picnicking in the park can work wonders!

ASK FOR AN ALLOWANCE

Ask for an allowance so that you can more easily take care of your personal life and preserve your privacy.

Asking for an allowance allows you to keep your private life private. Because your position takes you out and about so much, you'll inevitably need to tend to business and personal items in a very short period. Having an allowance on the phone and the vehicle means that you can more easily keep these two areas separate. Living in your own house allows you to entertain whenever you please. And that prevents charges of misuse of property!

Superintendents who *ask for an allowance* help themselves and their districts. When a phone, home, or vehicle is provided for the superintendent's use, the district ends up paying all the costs without getting the full benefit. Vehicle leasing fees, mileage payments, mortgages, phone plans, and the phone itself are all things that can be managed by selecting the right kind of usage for the superintendent. It also keeps the district away from public misperceptions that tax dollars are being wasted.

Ask for the allowance that fits your situation best. Some states don't allow districts to provide vehicles for their superintendents, so you'll have to track your miles and be reimbursed. Others provide a vehicle and allow for personal use to cut down on paperwork. If you have a choice in that district, use your own car and get reimbursed. Personal use of a public vehicle is considered taxable income by the IRS, and you'll end up filing extra paperwork every year. Do the same with your phone because who you call is nobody's business but your own!

ASK AN ATTORNEY

Ask an attorney to help you negotiate your contract.

Ask an attorney to guide you through the points of your contract before you sign. An attorney's experience will make you aware of points you might not have considered. It ensures that you understand your obligations and those of the district. Finally, the negotiation process sets the tone for the relationship with the board going forward!

Superintendents who *ask an attorney* end up more satisfied with the deal they've struck. Importantly, the contract can stipulate the types and number of professional development opportunities that will be paid by the board. An attorney can also discover how often the board will consider extensions and pay increases as well as the process they use for those items. The attorney will also know what the common negotiation points are in your state and will keep you from asking for things that are never offered.

Ask an attorney about the usual and unusual elements of your contract. Find out whether you'll be hiring other administrators or whether the board handles those positions; this tells you how much influence you'll be able to exert inside the schools. The salaries in surrounding districts will be another key piece of information, as will the types of benefits provided by those other districts. And because the attorney will have been in the community longer, he or she will know about economic and social elements that might impact your negotiation. Ask an attorney to create the best results!

VALUE VIDEO

Value video when you need to set up a meeting without disrupting schedules.

The *value of video* is enormously helpful with meetings. Videoconferencing has developed to the point where it's easy to use, so it's a great way to get everyone in the district comfortable using technology. And since videoconferences can be attended without leaving the building, all the attendees save time and expenses!

Value video because when it comes to districtwide initiatives, almost nothing is going to work better! Large projects take a lot of time to manage, and the level of details involved can unfortunately spin out of control. Videoconferencing allows savvy superintendents to check in on projects much more often than on-site meetings allow. The technology can also be used to split off smaller groups for their own meetings immediately after the entire group has met virtually.

Take full advantage of the *value of video* by using a free conferencing service, like Fuze, GoToMeeting, or MeetingBurner, all of which were rated as top free programs by Reviews.com. Encourage participants to enhance their presentations with PowerPoint or other slide show programs to really communicate effectively. And since most conferencing sites allow you to record the sessions, you'll have a permanent record of what was said that can be accessed by anyone in your district at any time.

DEVELOP, EVALUATE, AND DEVELOP

Develop, evaluate, and develop charts a course through a superintendent's evaluation.

Develop, evaluate, and develop creates an assessment that allows the superintendent to develop! When superintendents interact with the board about what an assessment will entail, they help the board feel more comfortable evaluating an educational professional. By the time the assessment rolls around, the lines of communication will be wide open. After the assessment has been completed, superintendents can use the feedback to develop their skills and abilities further.

Superintendents who *develop, evaluate, and develop* are the high achievers among their peers. They recognize that the assessment process provides multiple benefits. Developing the evaluation allows them to guide the board toward what really matters and away from less important areas. A strong evaluation can even enhance the bonus that might be provided. The manner in which feedback is given can reveal whether the superintendent is interacting well with the board during the rest of the year.

Develop, evaluate, and develop by recognizing that this process is collaborative. As with any other issue, you and the board are on the same side! Plan by defining performance expectations and areas of accountability. Ensure that systems are in place to offer real measurements of progress rather than someone's opinion on progress. Since the evaluation will consider the district's improvements, keep the board informed throughout the year about different milestones. And once you've received the evaluation, select one major and one minor area for your own growth. You'll become a superintendent superstar!

FRATERNIZING FAILS

Fraternizing fails the district, the community, and the position of superintendent.

Fraternizing fails because it has the potential to place employees in positions where they feel pressured or harassed. Their peers often see what's happening and begin to worry for their own well-being. When the community uncovers incidents of fraternizing, it loses trust in the individuals involved and the district as a whole. With so many fails involved, fraternizing is a fail that is easy enough to avoid.

Even superintendents in districts that don't prohibit relationships between employees discover that *fraternizing fails*. One Texas superintendent started a relationship with an employee in a different district. Although there were no rules in place to prevent the couple from coming together, the community raised questions about how that impacted the operations in each district. The board rushed to consider passing rules against fraternizing, and the entire event distracted from the efforts to provide solid academic training to the students.

Avoid *fraternizing failures* by having clear and consistent policies in your district. Even if surrounding districts haven't taken that step, shore up your own! Later, you can approach the leaders of other districts to discuss similar mandates. Because every person in your district can fall under public scrutiny, these policies ensure that the emotional snares created by intimate relationships don't harm your schools.

Iraheta, Adria. "YISD Considers Changing Fraternization Policy in Light of Superintendent's Relationship." KFOX14. September 16, 2016. Retrieved from http://kfoxtv.com/news/local/yisd-considers-changing-fraternization-policy-in-light-of-superintendents-relationship.

A SEPARATE PEACE

A separate peace prevents challenges by making funding sources clear.

A separate peace reminds superintendents to never commingle funds. A sharp focus on how money is handled prevents accusations of misconduct on the part of the district's employees. When transparency applies to funds, the parents and community members who are so important to schools know that everything is being done to further educational opportunities.

Superintendents can sometimes unintentionally disrupt *a separate peace*. In Maryland, a board and a superintendent were publicly attacked by their state senator over their use of resources. A nine-bus convoy was supposed to carry attendees to a demonstration against educational spending cuts. But that meant extra expenses, which the board intended to cover. The argument ended when the money was raised from contributions by the community, but the explosion could have been avoided by doing that up front.

Keeping *a separate peace* starts with one point that will be obvious to anyone at the superintendent's level: personal moneys should never mix with those of the schools. But it extends much further. Funds set aside for one project within a district should never be comingled with funds for other projects. In the same spirit, resources should never be coopted for a use for which they are not approved.

Goldreich, Samuel. "School Leaders Pass Hat to Cover Protest Convoy Cost." *Baltimore Sun.* January 12, 1992. Retrieved from http://articles.baltimoresun.com/1992-01-12/news/9213000329_1_harford-county-school-system-school-buses.

BRING IN THE BEST

Bring in the best when it comes to staffing decisions.

Bring in the best to create a high-functioning and responsive office. Every individual around you should know your expectations—and that you believe in his or her ability to deliver. Your attitude will create an atmosphere in which everyone on your staff strives to excel. And when everyone models their best for the district, the staff inside the schools will respond in kind!

Superintendents who *bring in the best* value human capital. Districts supposedly are organizations made up of schools, but really they're a conglomerate of people serving people. Since the product of that service is a well-educated and confident citizen, the result can come about only when individuals are inspired to help the next generation. Bringing in the best at your office is one of the best ways you can serve!

Bring in the best by attracting top talent from other states and districts. Provide every employee from your office down to the janitors with annual performance reviews. Ensure that every level of staff has access to the resources they need to improve on the jobs they're already doing well. And when you get the best, keep them! Build a culture of growth in your district that challenges top performers and provides satisfaction.

THE PREMISE OF A PROMISE

The premise of a promise is based on the trust that individuals have in your word.

The premise of a promise is built both by your position and by your actions. When you found all your words and actions on the trust that the district has in your ability, you prove to be the leader the district needs. The staff and the community can move forward with confidence knowing that any promise made is a promise that will be kept.

Superintendents understand that *the premise of a promise* is not the same as a contract. There is no legal obligation to stick to a promise. But if it is broken, the community and the staff will feel let down. They will view any promise made as a type of contract between the superintendent and the district. So be sure that the premise maintains the trust. Never make promises that can't be kept!

Maintain *the premise of a promise* by taking care with your words. Statements like "I guarantee" or "It will be done" can be heard as a promise. And when you do make promises, be sure that you know everything about how to deliver. Consider how scheduling changes might delay a time line, lock in the required resources, and put the right people in charge. Then you can maintain the trust that is the premise of everything you do as a superintendent.

STAND TALL

Stand tall because you won't be able to please everyone!

Standing tall broadcasts your confidence in your own decisions and skills. At times, you'll need to make unpopular calls. In certain districts, you might hear from a vocal minority who won't be pleased no matter what you do! Standing tall tells everyone that the naysayers can't win. The district and the community will thank you for having the strength to uphold what is best for the students.

Superintendent Kent Scribner knows what it means to *stand tall.* His district's policy is to accommodate transgender students by allowing them to use the restroom of the gender with which they identify. That brought no less a politician than the lieutenant governor down on his head! But the community and the board turned out in droves to support the superintendent and the policy. A former city council member went on record to call the politician a bully!

Stand tall first and foremost by knowing that you never have to explain your decisions. You do, however, need to keep the district and your community informed about the logic and reasoning behind those decisions. When you approach every interaction with this attitude, your calm confidence will help you penetrate all but the most obstinate naysayer's beliefs. Another important element is to know that things can change. Be flexible and change with them so that you can always stand tall!

"Fort Worth Superintendent Gains Allies over Transgender Bathroom Issue." *Dallas Morning News*. May 13, 2016. Retrieved from http://www.dallasnews.com/news/news/2016/05/13/fort-worth-superintendent-gains-allies-over-transgender-bathroom-issue.

BLEND WITH THE BOARD

Blend with the board to build and maintain trust and cooperation between you and the board.

Blending with the board ensures that both you and the board of education are able to perform your respective duties. Teamwork eliminates overlapping efforts and makes the district more efficient. Best of all, a strong relationship enhances the respect and communication that are so critical between you and the board.

Derrick Meador, the teaching expert for AboutEducation, feels that *blending with the board* is critical for a district's success. The superintendent, he notes, is the chief executive officer and "the face of the district." Because the role is so broad, superintendents are more responsible for a school's successes and failures than any other element. The board, on the other hand, is tasked with hiring the superintendent and providing oversight. They approve the superintendent's recommendations and provide mandates. "The best school districts," Meador says, "have boards of education and superintendents who work well together."

Your most important step in *blending with the board* is to set the district's priorities. This ensures that you hold the same vision and that you can more easily agree on which path to take. Setting priorities will allow you to create goals for the budget, educational programs, student services, and other key areas. Once the goals have been agreed on, you and the board can determine the milestones that should be reached, a time line for each milestone, and the accomplishments that should be achieved at each point. By setting priorities first, you'll both be better equipped to handle any issues or challenges that arise as the district travels down the road to success!

Meador, Derrick. "Examining the Role of an Effective School Superintendent." About Education.com. April 3, 2016. Retrieved from http://teaching.about.com/od/admin/a/Superintendent-Of-Schools.htm.

MAKE EFFECTIVE DECISIONS

Make effective decisions to stand by what you know is the best option.

Making effective decisions allows you to perform at your optimal level. When you are informed and aware of possible outcomes, you will automatically select the best path forward. The longer your track record of effective decisions becomes, the faster support will grow for your future decisions. Effectiveness breeds efficiency!

The Wallace Foundation believes that superintendents who *make effective decisions* are what's needed for real educational results. While classrooms can improve on their own, the real impact comes from high up at the district level. When the broader regulatory environment encourages and supports improvement, schools and students accelerate their progress.

Make effective decisions by combining intuition with reason. Intuition is really the wisdom you've gathered up over the years. You might not make conscious connections to every element of your past efforts, yet they are supporting your current efforts. Reasoning works on the conscious mind and allows you to analyze the information you have at hand. When you combine the two, decision making naturally results in effective and efficient outcomes.

REIN IN RISK

Rein in risk and reduce your district's exposure by measuring the potential benefits and losses of each decision.

Reining in risk reduces the negative impacts of decisions and actions. As a leader, you need to try new things. Calculating the risks and benefits involved with each activity guides you down the best path and returns the greatest benefits!

Rein in risk as a superintendent because innovation can be messy. Turning away from any potential for a negative outcome might seem like the best choice, but that eliminates any potential for the district to improve and grow. Take the chance on innovative new ideas by calculating risks and avoiding potential negative effects.

To *rein in risks*, balance innovation with your core goals. Look at both elements every time you need to make a change or enhance an area within your district. Evaluate everything critically by considering all the information you can gather about a situation. Determine what your desired return on investment—in terms of money, effort, time, and skill—will be. If there are no pathways to that return on investment, decline the project. And be ready to change course if a new pathway appears later that delivers that return!

MEET REALITY

Meet reality by being flexible enough to change plans based on current facts rather than past information.

Meeting reality allows you to be flexible and responsive to changing conditions inside your district. One of the key benefits is that you'll maintain productivity no matter what's happening in a school or in the community. Best of all, the big changes you make will result in smaller changes that trickle down to every level.

Superintendents in Georgia are *meeting reality* as it changes by pivoting away from testing. The new federal education law enacted in 2016 allows for greater flexibility in how testing is done. The Every Student Succeeds Act provides a way to pivot away from testing and instead focus on developing a well-rounded student body. The superintendents jumped on that and are leading the way!

Meet reality by meeting every situation where it is today. You'll always have to parse the information gathered in the past as well as the history of a certain event or activity. That's valuable information and shouldn't be jettisoned in the attempt to shift gears. But while holding the past in mind, consider where things stand today and, critically, where you want them to be tomorrow. Enhance your district's improvements and success by staying on top of things as they evolve!

FIRST YEAR EVERY YEAR

First year every year keeps you aware of first-year issues—even if you've been in the job for a decade!

First year every year keeps the new issues that crop up every academic year in balance. Achieve an understanding of your role's duties and balance them against what's actually possible. You'll suffer less from stress, build confidence in your abilities, and garner loyalty from the people who are most important to your district. When you recognize that every academic year is a first year, you'll continue building a foundation that will generate new successes for your students and your schools!

Superintendents think the first year is the toughest, but really the *first year is every year*. A kind of first year comes up every time the new academic calendar begins. Although experienced superintendents are comfortable with the public aspect of their roles, they can suddenly be thrust into intense scrutiny when the media pick up a hot topic. The political aspects of the job never stop churning, and the pathways to your goals are going to shift over time—making every year a first year.

Keep *first year every year* foremost in your mind by keeping your priorities and goals realistic. Recognize that continuous engagement with the public is a critical part of the job. Cultivate individuals you trust to be a sounding board according to their own background and experiences. When you balance the intense pressures with a reasonable and logical thought process, you'll triumph every year!

RISE ABOVE

Rise above the duties laid out in your job description to become a true leader.

Rise above the job description to energize yourself, your peers, and your community. When you go above and beyond, you inspire every administrator to rededicate themselves to the district's vision. Teachers recognize that you'll be there for them in good times and bad. Parents become confident that even the most vexing of long-term challenges will eventually be resolved. And in this scenario, the students receive the best their schools can offer!

Rising above the job description humanizes your role. It's the ultimate step for superintendents because they manage people, not districts. Academic achievement isn't the final goal; a student's education is. Teacher performance isn't a check mark on the list; a teacher's inspired passion checks off the whole list! Parents who have been hesitant to get involved make the time to volunteer. And every new task you complete adds to your self-worth!

The single largest thing you can do to *rise above* is to have a can-do attitude. Even challenges that have been chronic or that affect schools nationwide can be addressed or minimized. When you present a stable and determined approach to resolving these problems, intractable issues suddenly become obstacles that can be tackled. And because addressing one issue so frequently resolves portions of other issues, the attitude that lifts you above the job description will help you fulfill that job description at the same time!

DATA-DRIVEN DECISIONS

Data-driven decisions result in effective programs that enhance your district's progress.

Data-driven decisions create a culture of quality in your schools. Accurate data, when considered with the district's goals in mind, point out the areas that need adjustment. Improvements can be implemented in a timely fashion, and issues are resolved much earlier. Best of all, data-driven decisions support your efforts and allow you to proceed with confidence!

The National Center for Education Statistics champions *data-driven decisions*. In its tip sheet "Quality Data: The Role of the Superintendent," they note that superintendents should first consider how the district currently uses the data it gathers. Recognize that all the data gathered on educational programs and curricula can be used when applying for funding. By using data, superintendents can meet their responsibility to enhance educational programming and academic achievement.

Support your *data-driven decisions* by first ensuring that the information collected by your district is accurate. Be sure that all personnel, from teachers to data entry clerks, understand the vital role information plays in their schools. Then utilize the data to set educational benchmarks that can be measured and assessed. Technologies, like handheld devices and free software programs, can support effective and efficient data gathering. Finally, encourage your peers and administrators to make data-driven decisions of their own.

National Center for Education Statistics. *Forum Guide to Building a Culture of Quality Data: A School and District Resource* (NFES 2005–801). Washington, DC: U.S. Department of Education, National Center for Education Statistics.

RESPOND WITH PASSION

Respond with passion to ensure a long and prosperous career that provides real benefits for your district.

Responding with passion brings an intangible yet powerful element to your work. Every step you take will be buoyed by your drive and determination. Passion naturally creates an optimistic outlook, and that type of positive, forward-thinking, and future-focused attitude will infect your district with joy! The position of superintendent is more than a job. It's an adventure!

Although Superintendent Joseph McFarland thought his role leading the Derry Township district was only temporary, he quickly *responded with passion.* At first, he was turned off by the political aspects of the job. But when he stepped in to temporarily fill a vacancy, he discovered that those aspects weren't as onerous as he'd thought. On top of that, the teamwork and community building were so appealing that he wanted to become a superintendent on a permanent basis!

Respond with passion by remembering that your background and experience have led you to this exact place. You don't get to be superintendent without having jumped over some major hurdles. The goals you've worked so hard to achieve have built the skills and abilities required by your position. Now every one of them will be brought to bear on an entire district! That's a lot of lives to affect. You hold the future of every student, every school, and the entire community in your hands. What a great responsibility—and what a joyful task!

Mattera, Julianne. "Derry Township School Board Names Joseph McFarland as New Superintendent." PennLive.com. January 22, 2014. Retrieved from http://www.pennlive.com/midstate/index.ssf/2014/01/derry_township_school_board_na_2.html.

STRATEGIC DIRECTION

Strategic direction is your plan for a course of action that achieves your district's goals.

Strategic direction is the hallmark of effective leaders in education. The plans you lay down for different departments provide both the strategies required to achieve goals and the actions that will lead to success. When you provide strategic direction, your departments gain traction because every step they take propels them forward!

Superintendents usually offer *strategic direction* when they first step into their role at a particular district. Because they are new, everyone is waiting to discover exactly what the new leader's vision will entail. The pathway that is laid out often covers several years. But strategic direction can be applied to nearly every mandate or goal, even those that need only a few months to enact. Keep everyone on the right path by providing the strategies and the direction they need!

Providing *strategic direction* can seem a bit overwhelming, but it doesn't have to be. In fact, when you're announcing long-term (or even short-term) plans, a brief version will focus personnel on the goals, the primary milestones, and the benefits. This type of packaging ensures that your message is communicated clearly. It also allows you to inform departments that aren't involved in the project about the task, which creates cohesion across your district. Be clear, be succinct, and be the one to lead the charge!

THE INFORMATION HIGHWAY

The information highway provides clear and precise instructional methods based on data.

The information highway helps you determine the impact that current instructional methods have on students and points out the changes that need to be made. Student performance data can validate current methods and ensure that appropriate budgets are drawn up. Information about academic shortfalls can reveal gaps that need to be addressed. Best of all, data can be used to bring home your points when you communicate with teachers, administrators, and parents.

The most useful *information highway* isn't found in reams of data. Instead, it arrives in the form of meaningful details. Test scores that fall short in math don't tell you much about what's really going on. But data that come in during the school year about different grade levels' math performance will guide you through changes in specific schools, curricula, and teaching methods.

To make *the information highway* work for you, consider the sources from which you gather information. A diverse range of sources can reveal which procedures need adjustment more quickly because the shortfalls will show up multiple times. Compare your assessments to state and federal mandates to ensure that they align. Year-end data should be passed on to the teachers before the start of the following calendar year so that they can be prepared for the incoming grade's level of proficiency. Finally, use homework surveys, in-class spot checks, and other quick methods to take the pulse of your schools throughout the year.

PLUG DRAINS

Plug drains by eliminating waste and enhancing efficiency.

Plugging drains is one of the best ways to shore up shrinking budgets. When you target wasteful practices, you free up funds for more deserving activities. Often plugging financial drains also reduces staff hours, managerial issues, and scheduling troubles, so the approach offers benefits in many areas!

When Meridian Joint School District in Idaho wanted to increase the amount of funding it received through grants, it first had to *plug drains*. The district's teachers were struggling to fill out the applications, so although they spent a lot of time working on the forms, they didn't receive many grants. By hiring a part-time grant facilitator, the process became much more streamlined. For the next five years, the amount of funding the district received through grants increased every year!

Plug drains by using social media to crowdsource ideas from the entire district, including the community. Pull in resources from national nonprofits, like United Way and AmeriCorps, to locate volunteers who can fill lost positions, like academic coaches and intervention specialists. Use GPS routing software to cut transportation department costs. Pick up refurbished Apple devices through Mac to School. Every drain you plug allows you to route the savings to places where the money is really needed!

Molnar, Michele. "Idaho School District's Scarce Resources No Barrier to Innovation." Education Week Leaders to Learn From. February 24, 2015. Retrieved from http://leaders.edweek.org/profile/linda-l-clark-superintendent-fostering-innovation.

MEASURE WHAT MATTERS

Measure what matters to turn attention away from test scores and back to what truly counts.

Measuring what matters keeps the community from becoming obsessed with any slight change in test scores. Teachers will be inspired by the fact that their performance isn't being ranked according to a single number. Principals will feel more appreciated because much of what they do doesn't normally end up on a spreadsheet. And parents will recognize that you're right and will follow your lead!

Measuring what matters is especially important in an era of standards, mandates, and rankings. The learning that takes place in the classroom is what matters most to teachers. The safety of the school campus and the surrounding neighborhood matters to parents. The good citizens who graduate in your district matter to the community. Measuring these elements—and providing those data to the entire district—keeps the focus on what's really important.

Measure what matters by using information the district already gathers. Quarterly grades can show how much progress is happening in the classrooms and can be shared on social media. Graduation and attendance statistics can prove that your schools provide an environment that is inspiring, encouraging, and safe. Staff that take on new learning opportunities during breaks can model the lifelong learning your district wants to embed in its youth. Every day, you have a lot of opportunities to measure what matters!

EARLY WINS

Early wins give the district hope right out of the gate and spur its efforts over the long run.

Early wins are useful when superintendents first start out as well as at the beginning of a new project or calendar year. Parents are heartened by the progress that has been made so early in the game. The community recognizes that benefits will accrue during the entire project rather than only at the end. And the district's staff are motivated to continue the intensive efforts they've already put in!

Early wins are best accomplished by having a flexible approach. Every new project and each calendar year begins with a handful of primary and secondary goals to be accomplished on a specific schedule. When new methods or approaches promise to shorten the time line or achieve even better results, consider implementing them. Early wins ensure that your district will create even bigger wins!

At their most basic, *early wins* are really only milestones in a particular process. By celebrating each milestone as an achievement, superintendents can keep everyone engaged in the effort. It's easy to get buy-in for lofty goals like closing the education gap or increasing on-time graduation; it's far more difficult to keep all the players involved at a level that ensures success. Share early wins and subsequent wins to rekindle that passion!

HELP YOURSELF

Help yourself by tending to your own needs.

Of all the people involved in the district, superintendents are the ones who most need to *help themselves*. When you have the proper support network in place, you'll avoid a lot of the stress involved with your position. Helping yourself can make you feel supported and refresh your energy and passion!

Helping yourself puts you back in charge. Caring for yourself sends a powerful signal to your subconscious about the value that you provide to the district. Taking breaks throughout the day, utilizing your vacation time, and other forms of self-help build the inner strength to soldier on. No matter what type of situation or event pops up, you'll have the self-esteem and calm attitude needed to stay strong in the face of adversity.

Being constantly under fire (or feeling like you are) and managing crises can really wear you down. *Help yourself* by pulling together a small group of individuals you can speak with confidentially. Recognize that they don't need to be involved in education; they can be good friends or small-business owners who understand what it's like to be responsible for everything. Building a network of social support is a critical step that can truly help!

BRIDGE THE DIGITAL DIVIDE

Bridge the digital divide by building a 1:1 program that allows students to take the devices home.

Bridging the digital divide has a profound impact on underserved populations. A 1:1 program that assigns a dedicated digital tool to each student supports differentiated instruction and project-based learning. It also enhances communication and allows students to practice on the same tools they'll be expected to use when they graduate.

In order to fully *bridge the digital divide*, task teachers with considering whether homework assignments require Internet access. In 2013, a White House broadband report concluded that only 71 percent of Americans subscribed to high-speed Internet access. The adoption rate was even lower among African American and Hispanic households. To truly serve all students and to help close the education gap, encourage teachers to assign homework that can be downloaded at school and then accessed when students go home.

Bridge the digital divide by opting for devices that can be used just as well offline as online. Find out if any nonprofit groups are working with your local telecommunications providers to service families who qualify for free or low-cost lunch programs. Connect2Compete, which was available in forty-nine states in 2015, has a mission to provide access to all Americans who can't afford Internet services. Bridge the digital divide to carry all your students to academic success!

Goodman, Jessica. "The Digital Divide Is Still Leaving Americans Behind." Mashable.com. August 18, 2013. Retrieved from http://mashable.com/2013/08/18/digital-divide/#AHqFuCL8j5q3.

BUILD IT HIGHER

Build it higher utilizes what's already been created for better results!

Build it higher avoids some of the churning that can burden a district when new initiatives or changes seem to constantly come along. It eliminates the feeling that all the previous efforts to change will be wasted by "starting over again." Best of all, it emphasizes sustainable adjustments for sustainable benefits.

Build it higher applies to both the district and the community. Teachers and administrators might worry that new initiatives are going to supplant the projects they've worked so hard to create. The community can feel as if no one is listening when it's constantly asked what it wants. In both cases, superintendents who emphasize that past efforts are foundations for new initiatives will achieve buy-in much faster!

Build it higher by knowing exactly what has happened in the past. Utilize the core components of old programs to spin off new ones. Reallocate resources when you need to adjust a project's direction. Every change should be accompanied by a clear respect for what has come before. When you show people that the new efforts are small compared to the previous efforts, they recognize that change can be easily achieved. And when you clarify the benefits of the change, the new will rise quickly atop the old!

SHORE UP SAFETY

Shore up safety to provide a secure learning environment throughout your district.

Shoring up safety is a preventive step that can deflect a world of harm. Working with community partners on security efforts strengthens your ties to different stakeholders and comforts parents. Conflict resolution techniques result in a more stable student population with fewer behavioral issues. Your caring school community will impact with the larger community!

Shoring up safety works by preventing violence and creating a better response if violent events do occur. The same school resource officers who monitor the property to prevent dangerous activities are also some of the most important first responders! When a proactive security system is in place, every school in the district has a better chance at staying safe.

Shore up safety by calling on parents to form community watch programs in neighborhoods around each campus. Provide annual training for all staff in emergency response techniques. Ensure that each building in the district has a dedicated team that regularly reviews the emergency preparedness plan and can make adjustments as necessary. Finally, train teachers and staff on the best ways to support students in the event of a crisis.

DECOMPRESS DEMONSTRATIONS

Decompress demonstrations to defray the negative impact of walkouts and protests while giving your district a voice.

Decompressing demonstrations keeps your district on track—and it ensures that everyone in your district speaks in a way that can be heard! Students are given a credible way to voice their concerns without disrupting school schedules. The police don't have to be involved, and media coverage becomes much more favorable. Importantly, every individual in the district, from the youngest student to the oldest community member, knows they are safe inside the controlled environment provided by your schools.

In America, every individual has the right to free speech, so *decompressing demonstrations* is a key skill for superintendents. The most recent presidential election caused demonstrations during which hundreds of students walked out of dozens of schools nationwide. In some cases, such as the demonstration at a courthouse in Portland, Oregon, more than a hundred individuals were arrested. One protestor was shot by a fourteen-year-old boy. Because school students were present, they were also in danger.

Decompress demonstrations by staying ahead of the game. Teachers and staff should constantly feed information to your office about possible events. No tip is too small to follow up on! When you determine that an event is likely to occur, immediately notify your district and let it know that your directives will follow soon. Eliminate the event or at least reduce its size by offering educational components around the issue in classrooms, setting up digital and live forums in which students can speak, and telling students about the negative impact of a walkout or demonstration. It is important at this stage to work with any student or administrative leaders connected to the issue.

If the event can't be stopped, have a response team on hand and physically present hours before schools open. Have one or more representatives at or near the event to provide up-to-the-moment information. Deemphasize the rebellious nature of the act by vocalizing support for the right to protest and ensure that any students who leave class for the event also leave campus. Escort all students back to their classrooms once the event is over and have administrators and teachers engage students in a dialogue about the event.

Every moment of a planned demonstration is also an opportunity to diffuse its impact. By being proactive, you'll keep your district safe and operating smoothly.

"Students Walk Out of School, March through Portland (Live Updates)." *The Oregonian*/OregonLive. November 14, 2016. Retrieved from http://www.oregonlive.com/portland/index.ssf/2016/11/students_walk_out_of_school_pr.html.

CHANGE WITH THE TIMES

Change with the times to keep your district on the cutting edge!

Changing with the times allows your district to shift and transform when the need arises. You won't be caught behind the trends that will enhance academic achievement and staff satisfaction. Every opportunity will be grasped in the moment. Your district will never be sucked into a downward spiral if you stay focused on the next higher level!

Changing with the times is something that Boston-area superintendents want to do right now. Spurred by the need to provide high school students with more sleep, they have thrown their support behind starting the school day later. The shift would be small, moving the current starting times of 7:30 to 8:00 a.m.—only half an hour—but the change is supported by parents who want to enhance their teenagers' well-being.

Changing with the times calls for flexibility. You are already constantly looking for ways to enhance and improve operations, so changing with the times is right on track. Be aware of new educational research and theories that are being discussed in academic circles. Tap into the studies and see for yourself whether the results point to changes that will benefit your district. And be proactive about asking your network of peers about the ways they are changing with the times. You'll keep your district on the cutting edge!

Vaznis, James. "Suburban Boston Superintendents Favor Late High School Start Time." *Boston Globe*. March 29, 2016. Retrieved from https://www.bostonglobe.com/metro/2016/03/29/suburban-boston-superintendents-group-favors-later-high-school-start-time/8BdOOrfP03XP0CpuLxbchI/story.html.

Part III

Superintendents as Leaders

BRIEF THE BOARD

Brief the board to keep them up to date on important activities and goals.

As the board secretary, you are responsible for *briefing the board.* When they understand all the elements that go into your efforts, they are better equipped to adopt policies that support your activities. And since they incorporate the community's view on school programs, they provide you with another way to serve the district's students.

Briefing the board keeps you in touch. Whenever you communicate with that group of people, you are dealing with a single entity composed of individuals. Each member has his or her own ideas about what will work and what should be set aside. When you become their reliable source of information, they recognize the depth of your knowledge. They also realize that you respect them enough to keep them informed. With that powerful combination in hand, they will be open to your advice and opinions and will take action accordingly.

Brief the board regularly by setting up an e-mail list solely for them. Every few weeks, send them a quick e-mail with updates on all the various topics they will consider at their next meeting. Tell them where advances have been made, describe the issues causing setbacks (as well as the solutions you are implementing), and list upcoming projects and those on hold. This is your chance to offer additional short notes that reflect your professional opinions, which will strengthen your approach when it's time to garner more support. You also will spend less time reviewing those details later on, which will make your more direct interactions with the board more efficient!

TRUE TO TYPE

Being *true to type* as a superintendent focuses your approach on stabilization, innovation, or a blend of both.

Staying *true to type* helps you present a singular impression for your district and maintain a singular focus for your efforts. Your role encompasses a lot of duties, and each task should be organized under a single banner. At its most basic form, you're there either to stabilize the district or to create innovative opportunities for the district. A more complex form is to blend the two and ensure that progress occurs while nothing slips back or declines.

True to type supervisors provide the district with a cohesive approach. The more traditional superintendent will focus on the schools and the students, ensuring they get the resources they need and solving problems when they arise. One who is interested in reforms looks much more at data, organizational structures, and innovation. The blended approach takes the best from each to build schools that provide the best of the old and the new.

Stay *true to type* by knowing exactly what your district needs. Pull in every bit of information you can, including the opinions of your educators and community. Assess available resources, which include funds, equipment, property, and people. Then organize plans that include plenty of individual milestones against which progress can be measured. At every milestone, consider whether the plan is working out in a way that stays true to type. If not, make adjustments to bring the plan back on track!

LEAD BY EXAMPLE

Lead by example to get the most out of your district.

Leading by example provides everyone who works with you an exemplary model to emulate. When people see you doing whatever needs to be done for the good of the students, they become more proactive on their own. Remain unflinching before challenges to encourage strength and fortitude in your staff. Be bold and flexible to generate a resilient community. Your example will lift up your entire district!

Superintendents who *lead by example* achieve greatness! Superintendent Gary Martel of the Moody Independent School District calls it "witnessing the struggle." He goes out into his district to have lunch in school cafeterias, enjoys a morning coffee at a café where he can interact with local residents, and develops social relationships with administrators. When issues arise or people want to get involved, they know that they can approach him and be heard!

Lead by example in small steps that have a huge impact. Never ask your employees to do something you wouldn't do yourself. Pitch in on volunteer efforts at different schools whenever you have time. Implement sustainable practices, like recycling and energy efficiency, from the top down. And when you attend a program or conference that enhances your skills, share notes about what you learned with other administrators. Your every effort will become another example for others to follow.

PUT POLITICS ASIDE

Put politics aside to keep your district's focus on education—the only thing that counts.

Put politics aside to supercharge your efforts and your results. You'll keep your district from becoming the battleground of whatever issue a governor or senator wants to showcase. You'll safeguard your students and administrators from negative attention. Best of all, when you refuse to engage in the political storms that can overwhelm schools, you allow everyone in your district to feel comfortable doing the same!

One of the biggest reasons to *put politics aside* is made clearly visible by the groups that so often lead the charge for reform. Too often, these groups are put together—and controlled—by individuals who have no background in education or politics. Frequently they don't even have experience as leaders! Your entire district is founded on a system that delegates authority in a structured hierarchy. Loose cannons send shrapnel your way!

Put politics aside by ensuring that everyone who holds authority has an appropriate background that makes them a true fit. When groups approach your district with high-flying and incoherent reforms, reveal the ideological basis of their campaigns that prove that the reforms just won't work. Keep everyone focused on the students, their education, and the impact to the community!

CLEAN THE GRID

Clean the grid by creating an organizational chart that is clean, clear, and easy to understand.

Cleaning the grid ensures that everyone knows whom they report to and where to get help. Much more than a managerial tool, a good organizational chart can show parents, teachers, and community groups whom to contact about specific issues. A chart that is easy to use saves everyone time, allows information to flow better, and keeps everyone informed.

Superintendents who *clean the grid* send a clear message to their district: they are empowering every individual involved with education! An organizational chart shows parents, community groups, and even students how their schools work. It reveals exactly what is being done in their district every day to keep education on track. And because transparency is so important today, it builds trust in every person whose name appears on the chart.

Clean the grid by making the chart as simple as possible. Rather than showing everything on a single graphic, break out each school into its own chart. Then provide one graphic that shows how the board and superintendent fit into the overall hierarchy. To make sure that everyone at least glances at this valuable tool, run a contest for best graphic. Allow individuals (even students) to generate the charts using different colors, clip art, or photos. You'll get a lot of mileage out of the contest because so many people will end up with knowledge that they might not have sought out on their own!

LOCATE LEADERS

Locate leaders whose instructional and leadership capacities will carry your district to greatness!

Locating leaders is critical to a district's success. Each in their own way, the individual leaders you single out will inspire students, engage parents, empower teachers, and enable administrators. The myriad tasks that need to be accomplished will be completed more easily by teams guided by these leaders. You'll also have a far less challenging time gathering and disseminating information when you turn to those leaders!

Locating leaders allows you to delegate, and delegating enhances your sphere of influence! Since you can't be in every school at the same time, your leaders will keep you up to date about the latest developments, needs, and accomplishments. When those leaders pass some of those delegated tasks on to peers, the reach of the influence you have through those leaders increases. And since individual leaders all have different levels of connection with the wider community, they allow you to reach deeper into the community much more quickly than you could on your own.

Locate leaders by starting at home base. Look at your immediate staff and determine their individual ability to lead others or to head up a special task. Then consider who among each school's administrators would make a good leader. Eventually, you'll be able to pinpoint leaders in the broader community as well. Every time a new project develops or an ongoing one comes up for reassessment, consider whether one of those leaders might be the perfect choice. Then let them lead!

MENTOR FOR THE MOST

Mentor for the most out of your principals and yourself!

Mentoring for the most is a two-way street. When you mentor the principals in your district, you help them achieve goals and potentially can groom them for the position of superintendent. When you are mentored by an associate or through a program, your career success takes on a whole new trajectory! Trustworthiness, confidence, empathy, and a host of other benefits accrue to both mentor and mentee, so this step is one of the best.

Superintendents who *mentor for the most* get exactly what they want out of their administrators. First-year principals need all the advice they can get, so they're a perfect recipient. Principals who have been in the job for a while can hit the reset button on their motivation and on their approach. Even senior principals can learn something new!

When principals continue to learn and grow, your district achieves at the highest possible level.

Mentor for the most by determining how much time you can devote to this task. Then select one or two individuals who either need or want your assistance. As you build a relationship with each person, you'll find that he or she will use less of your time. Devote that extra time to another individual—or use it to establish a relationship with a mentor of your own! Remember to check in regularly. Mentors are often the ones to initiate contact because the mentee truly respects your time. Let them know you are available by dropping a quick e-mail every month.

PRIVATE AND PUBLIC

Private and public considers how your approach to an issue might change based on the board's response.

The *private and public* elements of your position can make the process of handling issues rocky or smooth. Know ahead of time which issues will be discussed behind closed doors and which will be hashed out in public to help you negotiate sticky situations. And because board members might behave differently in each situation, understanding how their responses might change allows you to prepare appropriately.

Private and public approaches might change depending on the district in which you've landed. Generally, however, issues relating to personnel, any type of litigation, and a handful of other areas will be conducted in private. All other issues will be conducted in meetings that are open to the public. That includes the media, so take special care with your attitude and your words whenever you step into a public venue.

Determine which matters are *private and public* before you step into your office for the first time. Review your district's rules so that you will constantly be aware of how you can handle challenges. While you can certainly be more frank in private meetings, know that it takes only one board member who doesn't get their way to leak information to the community. So keep your emotions in check when you speak your mind. Your professionalism will ensure that, no matter what, you are beyond reproach.

INCENTIVIZE TO CLARIFY

Incentivize to clarify goals and the steps needed to reach those goals.

Incentivize to clarify ensures that everyone in the district is aware of the short- and long-term goals for each school. Drawing attention to specific areas with incentive programs keeps everyone focused on success! And because they're driven to rack up those rewards, they'll spend time thinking through how to meet those goals. Harness many minds to generate creative and unique solutions.

Incentivize to clarify an issue that impacts nearly every school in the nation: attendance. A comprehensive approach allows your outreach to dig deep into the community and especially into homes that tend to have the least contact with schools. When incentives, like outings for classes that have the best monthly or quarterly attendance rates, are provided, the push to enhance those numbers takes on a positive tone!

Incentivize to clarify at every level in your district. Provide students with free and low-cost rewards, like being allowed to help in a different classroom at the elementary level or a homework-free night for a high school classroom. Teachers might be offered a day with their principal as their classroom helper! When your staff have to work late, invite their family members to join them in the office for the dinner break. The incentives are limitless, as are the benefits!

NIX THE NEPOTISM

Nix the nepotism—and even the appearance of nepotism—to maintain your reputation.

Superintendents hold a high position in education and must take care to *nix the nepotism*. When superintendents are viewed as fair and equitable, their reputations gain the luster of ethical strength. The people who work with them and around them become loyal allies even when things aren't going well.

In the past few years, superintendents—as well as their districts—suffered when they failed to *nix the nepotism*. The *Chicago Tribune* uncovered a number of area superintendents who hired relatives in their own districts. Although Illinois doesn't prohibit boards from hiring family members of their own or other districts, the media and the public made their disapproval known. A board meeting on the issue revealed a divided audience. Districts have enough to worry about without these kinds of questions arising!

Nix the nepotism by knowing up front whether your state allows relatives to be hired. When the candidate being considered is a friend or associate, inform the board clearly about how you are connected. Most professional associates won't cause problems; making referrals in those cases is actually good for your district. But if it's a friend or someone you know on a casual basis, consider how it might look to others before you put a name forward. The closer your relationship to that person, the more potential there is for doubt. Tread carefully, and you'll stay out of the swamp!

Gaines, Lee V. "In Wake of D219 Investigation, Firm Suggests Anti-Nepotism, Confidential Reporting Policies." *Chicago Tribune*. April 18, 2016. Retrieved from http://www.chicagotribune.com/suburbs/skokie/news/ct-skr-district-219-investigation-records-tl-0421-20160418-story.html.

REPRESENT

Represent your district by being aware of little things that can trip up even a sterling superintendent.

Superintendents who *represent* the utmost in their behavior prove their worth every moment of every day—even during moments that for other people are private. Representing during "off-duty" hours provides the community with a picture of the whole person—a person they can trust. By keeping your standards of conduct high even when you're relaxing with the board, you'll prove that their original choice and their continued faith in you is well placed.

When a superintendent in New York failed to *represent*, his embezzlement of more than a million dollars was uncovered. For years, he had driven expensive cars and given his administrators expensive gifts. Considering that his salary was $200,000, no one thought much of it. But when the embezzlement was uncovered, the community realized that his spending had come at the expense of the district.

Represent your community by making wise choices. Never accept kickbacks or bribes and be wary about accepting gifts that might be misconstrued as something more. Don't regularly frequent bars and consider buying your alcohol in a different county. It's fine to buy whatever you enjoy with your salary but refrain from bragging about it to avoid suspicions that you're spending more than you make. Remember that everything you do or say is subject to being recorded by a cell phone or other device. Represent the best of who you are!

Kolker, Robert. "The Bad Superintendent." *New York* magazine. March 9, 2013. Retrieved from http://nymag.com/nymetro/urban/features/9908.

24/7/365

24/7/365 defines every superintendent's schedule.

24/7/365 reflects your commitment to be the chief executive of your district. The duties that require your presence during evenings, weekends, and holidays are opportunities to prove your dedication. They also allow you to interact and connect with individuals you might otherwise never meet.

Being available *24/7/365* is a tall order, but it's an expected part of the job. A superintendent's salary is high precisely because the job is so demanding. Boards put a lot of time and effort into finding the right candidate, and the community wants to know that the person in charge is going to deliver the best. As a leader, you must provide around-the-clock availability to the district with the security and confidence it truly needs.

24/7/365 is an expectation that can be easily met with digital devices. Set your smartphone ring tones to different sounds so that you'll always know when you must answer a call. Ensure that everyone knows the fastest way to connect with you: by e-mail, with a call, or with a text. Set up a special e-mail account for emergency situations only and have your smartphone notify you whenever an e-mail arrives in that box. To ensure that you aren't waylaid by frivolous requests during your off-hours, practice saying, "I need to be in my office to help you with that. Can you contact me tomorrow during work hours?"

THERE WILL BE HATERS

There will be haters whose vitriol has nothing to do with you or your performance.

Remembering that *there will be haters* helps you maintain a stable course. No matter what you hear, you'll be able to stay calm and present a collected, professional response. And because haters are usually individuals who are frustrated with their lives, you'll extend compassion and courtesy to people who really need it!

There will be haters in a superintendent's path. The position holds a high profile in the community and is prone to attack from just about everyone—even those who have zero understanding of educational and district policies. Recognize that these types of people often function with little information or incorrect information.

There will be haters, so prepare by understanding your own psychological reaction. It's natural to feel an emotional stab no matter how easygoing you are. Just allow that emotion to come up and move past it. Then turn the attention back to the actual issue. Move on politely: ignore nasty comments on social media, thank individuals who send in ranting e-mails for voicing their opinions, and confirm that you've heard someone in an open meeting before returning to the topic. You'll prove your valor under fire and garner even stronger support from your community!

THE DIPLOMATIC TOUCH

The diplomatic touch helps you respond in an appropriate manner.

The diplomatic touch is one of the most effective communication tools you can employ. It allows you to persuade effectively and assert your stance without being overbearing. You'll develop respect while showing that you respect others. And no matter how stressful an effort becomes, you'll find a successful outcome!

In *The School Superintendent: Theory, Practice, and Cases*, author Theodore Kowalski notes that *the diplomatic touch* can help when it comes time to provide support. Not every group or individual is open to receiving assistance; they might feel like they have failed if they accept help, or they might not think they need any help! At these times, advice or assistance that is provided in subtle and diplomatic matter can resolve the issue and result in improvements.

The diplomatic touch is actually the art of being tactful. Diplomacy arises when the superintendent understands that others might be sensitive to challenges to their beliefs, ideas, or feelings. Pay attention to body language to get additional clues. Always consider who you're speaking with and keep their own history and experiences in mind. What works with one person might not work with the next person. Diplomacy leads you to the best choice!

A CLEAR VIEW

A clear view looks out on a vision that you can promote.

A clear view provides the detailed information about the vision you have for your district. Since your clarity will allow you to communicate more effectively, buy-in from the board and the community will arrive much more rapidly. You'll inspire loyalty and confidence in your ability to build that vision in your district.

Superintendents who have *a clear view* lead the pack. The Southwest Educational Development Laboratory notes that no matter whether you're championing a new instructional method or spearheading a school improvement campaign, the vision a superintendent holds can make a real difference.

Create and maintain *a clear view* by considering where your district is now and where you want it to go. List the challenges being faced today and ones that might crop up as you move forward. Then determine how solutions to those challenges might move you closer to your vision. Practice communicating that vision by writing down brief ways to talk about it. Once you're able to naturally discuss the elements associated with your vision, you'll achieve exactly the success you envision!

EASE INTO EAGERNESS

Ease into eagerness to avoid seeming overconfident or judgmental.

Easing into eagerness helps you avoid the most common mistakes leaders can make. It prevents you from seeming like a "my way or the highway" ruler who won't listen to other people's opinions. It maintains open channels of communication. It also allows others to take the lead and relieve you of at least a small part of the work!

Ease into eagerness by avoiding the classic missteps of new school superintendents. In addition to being open and approachable, don't hand down a new ruling every time an individual makes a mistake. If someone breaks a commonsense rule like using school resources for personal activities, don't respond by implementing a districtwide regulation. The regulation will only insult all the people who give their best every day.

Ease into eagerness by throwing your door wide open! Invite—and listen to—the perspectives, opinions, and ideas of others. When questions or doubts arise about programs, turn the situation around and ask the entire district what it thinks should be done. You don't have to rule by consensus, but the ability of every voice to be heard and respected will result in a lot more support!

GROW TO GLOW

Grow to glow enhances your skills and, by extension, your district!

Grow to glow compounds the leadership skills you already possess. When you continue learning, you enhance your capacity to work effectively and efficiently. You also add new skills to your personal toolbox, which pays rewards for your career and everyone touched by your district. Superintendents who grow will glow!

The type of programs offered by graduate-level university training programs for superintendents proves that *growing to glow* is a valuable approach. Administrators have to complete courses in leadership, organizational theory, management, curriculum and instruction, school planning, and community relations. Any of these areas can have a huge impact. Efforts to grow in these areas will make a superintendent glow with success!

Grow to glow by taking advantage of the continuing professional education courses required for administrators. Join study groups to discover the most recent approaches and ideas being tested in education. Connect with scholars who focus on university-level graduate and post-graduate academic operations to see whether you can modify programs to fit your district. And reach out! Regular dialogue with peers can introduce you to new opportunities to grow and truly glow!

THE DOOR IS NOW OPEN

The door is now open enhances communication without becoming overwhelming.

The door is now open allows you to have an open-door policy—at specific times. You need to solicit feedback to gather information, and you want the community to know that they can approach your office. By opening the door at certain times, you control when and how information arrives and prevent your office from being overwhelmed by miscellany.

Leave behind a free-flowing exchange in favor of *a door that is now open*. Traditional open-door policies can kill productivity and turn employees into dependents who can't make their own decisions. Instead, allowing people to approach you during preset times gives you control of your schedule. It also encourages others to find solutions to the smaller issues that don't really need your input!

Prop *the door open now* by laying down ground rules. Let people know what types of situations are true crises that demand your immediate attention. Make sure everyone knows the chain of command so that other issues can be shuttled to other people. Touch base with your people on a regular basis to build rapport—and to allow most of the lingering issues to be handled at that time. And when you prop that door open, give your full attention to individuals who make use of it. Respect will flow both ways!

STAY IN STEP

Stay in step so that your actions match your words.

Stay in step with what you've said and match your actions to your words. Everyone in your district follows you—not your position, not your office, but you, the person. Your position as a leader is great, but you still have to earn respect, trust, and loyalty. Matching your actions to your words keeps them in step with you!

Superintendents absolutely must *stay in step* for one simple reason: they are leaders who are scrutinized from every angle. The parents in your district are going to parse every word you say about academic goals. Teachers and administrators will examine your recommendations on the curriculum. Politicians who are in the game for themselves will use you as a target. And the media won't always support your ideas. When your actions stay in step with your words, you'll become much less vulnerable to doubts and criticism.

Stay in step by defaulting to tactful honesty. When you speak the truth, you will be recognized as a courageous leader who is not afraid to tackle the big issues. Be clear about what you need and be even clearer when discussing your vision for the district and the values you expect the schools to uphold. Every moment of staying in step generates an operation that runs forward smoothly—and that will outrun its competitors!

THE PSYCHOLOGY OF POWER

Understanding *the psychology of power* helps superintendents feel connected!

The psychology of power can have a huge impact on a superintendent, so understanding it can allow individuals to make real and lasting connections. Handling your own psychological response to power keeps your gratitude and your ability to reciprocate kindness alive. When you know how to avoid the negative effects of handling power, you stay in control of the things that count!

The psychology of power is important for every leader to understand. Being in power can complicate relationships in many ways, all of which detract from effective leadership. But they all boil down to a single core: loss of trust. If you're suspicious of every nice thing a peer or subordinate does for you, your job is going to become a lot tougher!

The psychology of power doesn't have to corrupt your relationships. Work hard to bolster your trust in others. Set aside cynical thoughts and consider whether the person who's helping out is simply a kind and generous soul. Even if the act seems to be self-serving, if the action provides you with an advantage, say, "Thank you!" Make sure that you don't carry the power of your position over into relationships that form outside of work. When you become conscious and aware of who people really are, you'll be able to accept their friendship and their help—and you'll never feel lonely at the top!

ACE ACCOUNTABILITY

Ace accountability because as the chief executive, you really are responsible for everything in your district!

Ace accountability to achieve exceptional career and district results. By taking full responsibility, you ensure that your office is operating at full capacity. Your influence spreads to even the most remote parts of your district where your influence might otherwise not have its intended impact. Best of all, you'll model the type of behavior you expect from everyone associated with the schools!

Ace accountability at all times. A superintendent liaisons with the board, the community, and the schools and truly is the one responsible for keeping everyone informed and all systems working in tandem. When you place the mistakes of the district in your court, no matter where the flaw originated, you'll shore up cracks before they become chasms. Best of all, the district will be much more likely to funnel praise and credit your way—which you should also accept!

Ace accountability by actively seeking out responsibility. This might sound counterintuitive considering how much work is on your plate, but this isn't about performing more tasks. Instead, it's about communicating clearly, repeatedly, and consistently that you are the single person with ultimate responsibility. Even when the media are raking someone else over the coals, stand in front of them. Be their shield, and you'll build loyalty from the bottom to the second in command!

INFLUENCE IS POWER

Influence is power within the community, so identify the power brokers.

Influence is power for any superintendent who needs to negotiate a school district. By identifying the power brokers, you'll be able to cultivate relationships that make your job much easier. Pulling in support from key influencers pulls in support from a much wider swath of people. When you know who among the teachers, administrators, parents, and community members holds power, you harness that power for the good of the district!

Influence is power in the public school system. The key influencers are school boards, superintendents, community leaders, and teachers. Deal effectively with these individuals by becoming involved wherever these people get together. Meetings, social gatherings, and conferences are all events during which a trusting relationship can be built. Once trust has been established, utilizing the power brokers' influence becomes much easier!

Turn *influence into power* by starting with the people closest to you. Watch their activity levels to discover who is most engaged with the community, the board, and each school. Then find out who they know. Ask for introductions to key influencers in each arena. When you meet influencers, be sure to offer something of value. Engage in a friendly conversation about their primary area of interest, which will most likely be the area in which they hold influence. Offer new information or discuss how your own efforts advance that subject within your district.

Soon you'll have the attention of the key influencers—and they will be ready to go to work when you need them!

TOUGHEN UP

Toughen up so that you can make the hard choices—and then stand by your decisions!

Toughen up to get the greatest impact for every decision. Shying away from difficult issues doesn't serve students or schools. Instead, allow the razor of your logic to slice away the emotional elements, and you'll arrive at the core of the issue. You'll have a clear perspective and a precise understanding of what needs to be done. Then, because you know it's the right thing to do, it will be done!

Toughen up is a real-world requirement in a job that calls on you to allocate limited resources and sometimes take an unpopular stance. You'll be called on to make decisions that involve people's values and the dearest thing to their hearts: their children. The political aspects of your position can snarl how people view your office. In every case, making the tough choices will prove to be the correct choices when your schools and your district hit their stride.

Toughen up by asking always whether a decision will benefit your district. New initiatives need to offer clear and direct benefits for students or teachers. Outreach needs to penetrate sectors of the community where work hours or other difficulties prevent parents from getting involved. Resources need to be allocated to the administrative tasks that keep the schools operating in a fiscally and academically sound manner. If the tough decision will ultimately create rich learning opportunities, meet high expectations, and foster an atmosphere where quality is the daily goal, then there's really nothing tough about making that decision!

LEAD INSTRUCTIONAL LEADERS

Lead instructional leaders to provide students, teachers, and parents with a cutting-edge education!

Because superintendents lead the principals of their schools, they already *lead instructional leaders*. Superintendents who step up to the role of instructional leader step closer to the day-to-day activities of their district. They connect directly to the issues and concerns of the students and teachers who are in the academic trenches. And parents who recognize superintendents as instructional leaders will more readily engage them—and their principals—in dialogues.

Superintendent Liz Schott of the Kentfield School District found that just considering how she might *lead the instructional leaders* made her feel more connected to her district's educational programming. After attending Edutopia's Curriculum and Instruction Steering Committee Leadership Symposium, she was reminded that what really matters in schools is what happens in the classroom.

Lead the instructional leaders by talking to superintendents in nearby districts about what helps their students. When you share your district's triumphs, you'll return the favor! By comparing how different districts approach problems, create safe spaces, and engage curricula, you'll discover new and unique ways to help your students and teachers grow. Schedule time to visit your schools and get permission from other superintendents to visit theirs. Be sure to engage your principals in the same way. Let collective intelligence make you a leader of instructional leaders!

Schott, Liz. "Superintendent as Instructional Leader?" *Edutopia*. March 12, 2015. Retrieved from http://www.edutopia.org/discussion/superintendent-instructional-leader.

CONTINUITY COUNTS

Continuity counts in education as a whole and in your district in particular.

Continuity counts because it provides your district with stability. An environment that remains consistent feels safe for everyone involved. When people feel safe, they relax enough to turn their full focus toward the district's goals. Everyone from the bottom up knows there won't be any terrible surprises when they walk into the schools!

The Harvard Family Research Project found that *continuity counts* across settings and time periods. When students are given the opportunity to expand their learning during breaks and before and after school, the additional programs complement and support what they learn in class. Academic success can be boosted so much that expanded learning opportunities are recommended as a way to close the education gap!

Continuity counts in educational activities and administrative procedures. Make sure that everyone shares the same goals so that a continuity of purpose drives your district forward. Organize curricula across grades to build a sound educational platform from which graduates can launch their lives. And when things change, create continuity by pointing out how the goals, values, and purpose of the district still apply to the new methods. Continuity allows for continuous success!

Harris, Erin, and Wallace, Ashley. "Year-Round Learning: Continuity in Education across Setting and Time through Expanded Learning." NCSL and Harvard Family Research Project. December 2012. Retrieved from http://www.hfrp.org/publications-resources/publications-series/ncsl-harvard-family-research-project-brief-series-elo-research-policy-practice/year-round-learning-continuity-in-education-across-settings-and-time-through-expanded-learning-opportunities.

ROLES DEFINE GOALS

For everyone involved in your district, *roles define goals*.

When *roles define goals*, everyone becomes clear about their duties and their path forward. Individuals understand that they have a specific task to fulfill in order to reach the district's larger goals. And because the goals defined by roles are based on specific skills and experiences, everyone feels competent to perform at their peak ability!

Roles define goals through the district. The role of the parent is to care for the students in all aspects of life. The goal of the teacher is to create an environment in which learning can take place. Administrators are tasked with providing the resources students and teachers require, while the community has the goal of supporting every activity on which public education depends.

Roles define goals that are tactile as well as those that are intangible. Superintendents therefore have to pay attention to both material resources and psychological support mechanisms. In both instances, human resources are the answer. Pull in key support groups from the community so that the people in your schools have safe places to share. Ensure that the goals defined by each role are communicated directly to each individual at the beginning of each year. And when roles change, determine whether the goals have also shifted. When every individual meets the goals spelled out by their roles, the district becomes an educational powerhouse!

USE THEIR WORDS

When communicating with the different levels involved in your district and the community, *use their words*, not yours!

Using the words that your audience understands allows you to communicate clearly and effectively. Because your language will mirror their own, using their words helps you form and nurture relationships. Messages that are delivered in language that is easy to understand helps your district reach its goals.

The National PTA found that *using their words* can have an astonishing impact on parental involvement. In a study they conducted of 25,000 educational leaders, 89 percent said that one of the top reasons parents don't get involved is that they don't understand how to get involved! Ensure that all communications with parents and the wider community are conducted in the language that is "native" to their region.

When you want to *use the language* of your community, consider the average education level of the citizens. Superintendents often have advanced degrees, so their default language is often far too complex for people to grasp easily. Additionally, an experienced educator might use too many insider terms that people outside of education don't understand. Drop the acronyms, eliminate the jargon, and just talk to them like you would to a friend.

"Eleven Tips for Savvy Superintendents." National School Public Relations Association. February 2008. Retrieved from https://www.nspra.org/files/docs/SavvySuperintendents.pdf.

SOUND BITES

Sound bites and media training can help superintendents communicate with their districts.

Sound bites keep your message short and focused on the issue. Superintendents who learn to speak in bullet points can garner more support, shorten the amount of time consumed by communicating with others, and achieve buy-in much more rapidly.

Sound bites should be used by all educators in your district. When the message is delivered in ways that utilize traditional public relations tactics, the district is much more likely to receive coverage by the media. Every placement of your district's message in newspapers or television provides you with awareness, communication, and buy-in at zero cost!

Sound bites aren't that hard to master. Whenever you're about to disseminate a message, list the top two to four points you want to emphasize. Then expand on each point by writing a brief description that is two or three sentences long. The sentences should be simple and short. If you are going into a meeting or an interview where you'll be asked questions, recognize that the questions might head off in directions that aren't going to serve your district. Whenever possible, answer the question by circling back to one of those key points.

LEAD WITH CHARACTER

Lead with character to distinguish yourself as a leading superintendent.

Leading with character broadcasts the values that you will uphold for your entire district. It communicates the high expectations you have for yourself and everyone involved with the schools. Because character is based on an individual's essential spirit, leading with character allows people who haven't met you to feel as if they know you—and that creates strong bonds and inspires loyalty.

Superintendents who *lead with character* become true leaders. Everything about your attitude will convey the hopes, positivity, and enthusiasm you have for your district. That kind of approach is inspiring to individuals who might sink without a role model to emulate. And because character conveys the ultimate in ethical values, the district will work hard to build on those values.

Even individuals who don't have an ingrained talent for leadership can take the helm when they *lead with character*. Rather than presenting a hard-nosed or exacting personality, lead with the essence of who you are inside. Call on your compassion, your fortitude, and your integrity to guide the district. And be sure to call on your sense of humor! When you lead with who you truly are, your character comes to the forefront and makes your job that much easier.

SYSTEMIC THINKING

Systemic thinking examines the relationships between different components of the district.

Systemic thinking, first and foremost, helps you understand the ways the different elements of your district interact. Once these relationships are defined, the impact each has on the other (and on the district as a whole) can be defined. Systemic thinking provides a perspective that can be as broad or as detailed as needed when addressing a specific issue.

Systemic thinking is all but a requirement for superintendents. Even a small school district contains a vast number of groups and elements, all of which need to interact with each other in service of the whole. Policies, processes, practices, and people all become much more manageable under a superintendent who utilizes systemic thinking.

Integrate *systemic thinking* by recognizing that no school or group inside your district is an enclosed entity. Every campus and demographic is in some type of relationship with many other areas of the district. Even the district as a whole isn't a closed environment because what happens in one district can impact another. Stay in touch with key individuals so they can update you on new developments under their purview. Then all departments, groups, and individuals can work together more efficiently.

THE ETHICAL SHEPHERD

Superintendents who practice stewardship become their district's *ethical shepherd.*

The role of *the ethical shepherd* is part and parcel of a superintendent's job. Responsible planning and careful resource management provide the best stewardship of everything that has been entrusted to your care. It fulfills your obligations to the district in the best possible manner and allows you to keep the well-being of the district at the forefront of your vision.

The ethical shepherd embodies the unique position that superintendents have as educational leaders. By practicing responsible stewardship, they reveal all that is good about public education. They lead students to academic success, shepherd parents through supporting their children's education, and guide the community so that it can raise capable, responsible citizens. And because ethical shepherds are so well positioned with key influencers, they can provide the perspective that a board might be missing.

Become *the ethical shepherd* by building a cooperative system for your district. Rather than placing yourself or the board above parents, educators, and the community, link everyone together in a chain that becomes stronger at every junction. Build relationships so that you can delegate differing levels of authority and assign tasks to the groups that can handle them best. When you function as the ethical shepherd, your flock grows stronger!

CREATE A CULTURE

Create a culture within your district to promote cohesion.

Creating a culture within your district enhances daily operations by generating a cohesive driving force. A culture that pulls together all the diverse elements of a school district works like a rallying cry! Individuals participate in a trusting environment to achieve a shared vision. And that kind of culture is a collaborative culture!

Creating a culture is less about what you do and more about how you do it. In essence, every project and change, no matter how large or small, is going to become part of the culture if it applies to a shared vision. Your high expectations strengthen the value of that shared vision, and your trust in the ability of your district to succeed generates a trust in your ability to lead the district to that success. The culture drives everything toward the goals!

Create a culture by engaging in small-group discussions with community members. Interview staff to determine their needs and to tease out their ideas. This type of collaboration between you and others builds trust, opens channels of communication, and develops loyalty. Then task key individuals among your staff to do the same with parents and the larger community. The small-group format and individual discussions are powerful proof that your office is listening to every word! Your district's community will come alive with participation, ideas, and enthusiasm!

Final Words

ALWAYS A SUPERINTENDENT

Always a superintendent means that you are the chief executive officer, leader, and cheerleader for your district!

Always being a superintendent provides your district with your best efforts and brightest ideas. It makes you the admiral of a fleet that sails the educational waters during calm times and who pilots the fleet through storms. You are the head teacher, the lead administrator, the guide for the PTO, and the primary influencer in your community. When you succeed in one area, you also succeed in all the rest!

Thomas Tucker, the School Superintendents Association's National Superintendent of the Year for 2016, is an excellent example of someone who is *always a superintendent*. When he was young, his grandfather told him to never forget where he came from—and to always remember the struggles he'd conquered. Life's lessons taught him not only the value of an education but also how the gap between boys and girls and between middle-class and low-income students affects academic achievement. He worked to close that gap by lifting up his community along with the schools.

Live the motto *always a superintendent* by building a superintendent's lifestyle! Every moment, reach out to the community to build your relationships with others—and to connect groups and individuals. Every small thing you do to help a parent or citizen help him- or herself feeds back into the community as a whole and the schools in particular.

By creating a community of love through your actions and examples, you generate a better life for you, your schools, and everyone involved with your district. Make *always a superintendent* your rallying cry, and your district will always be first at the finish line!

Riede, Paul. "Remember Your Past and Pay It Forward." School Superintendents Association. May 2016. Retrieved from http://www.aasa.org/content.aspx?id=39386.

About the Author

For forty-three years, **Dr. Barbara D. Culp** has dedicated herself to education. After teaching at the elementary and middle school levels, she became the principal of a large elementary school and was selected as Principal of the Year. Currently, she is a part-time clinical supervisor for Brenau University's School of Education; she recently founded a tutorial service company for public, private, charter, and parochial schools. Dr. Culp graduated from Morris Brown College and Atlanta University with a master's degree and an EdD degree in administration and supervision. In addition, she graduated from the rigorous two-year Georgia Superintendent Professional Development Program. She has conducted workshops and training programs on classroom management and differentiated instruction.